Cancer causes anguish to so many. And yet there is .... their family and friends. This hope is the result of the continuing work done by the ......cer Research Campaign, and to enable such work to go on, it is essential that we should be untiring in our fundraising efforts. When funds can be raised at the same time as pleasure given by the contents of a cook book such as this, the Celebrity Cook Book, *then it is doubly worthwhile.*

Claire Macdonald of Macdonald

Cancer does not discriminate. It can affect the young, the old, male and female. It does not acknowledge geographical boundaries or material wealth. Relatives and friends of cancer victims share the suffering.

The fight against cancer must continue. This is why the Cancer Research Campaign deserves all the support we can give it.

The Lord Taylor of Warwick

We are all touched by the scourge of cancer in one way or another and want so much to fight it. We know only too well that the only way to conduct this campaign is through massive effort and we are daily reminded to keep up this pressure through the rewarding work carried out by Cancer Research Campaign.

The Lumsden Twins

Oddly enough, nobody in my family has ever suffered from cancer, on either my father or my mother's side. Of course, there is always time for a first, but those of us who remain untroubled have an added responsibility to help cancer research, or so I feel.

Auberon Waugh

Cancer Research Campaign

Celebrity Cook Book

Compiled and edited by
Belinda Pinckney

for the
75th anniversary of the
Cancer Research Campaign

Registered Charity Number 225838

Published by the Cancer Research Campaign,
10 Cambridge Terrace, London NW1 4JL
Registered Charity Number 225838

First published 1998

Printed in England by Beshara Press, Beshara House,
Northway Lane, Tewkesbury GL20 8JH

ISBN 0-9508422-5-7

cancer
research
campaign

Making Cancer History
75th Anniversary
1923–1998

The Cancer Research Campaign was launched in May 1923 with a
gift of £20,000 from Sir Richard Garton. Since that date the Campaign
has funded research carried out by individual scientists and
scientific organisations.

The Cancer Research Campaign funds about a third of all cancer
research in the UK. This amounts to spending in the region of
£50 million in 1998. The Campaign is the major funder of research
programmes in universities and medical schools and is one of
the largest medical charities in the UK.

The Campaign supports a broad programme of research to find
better and more effective ways to prevent and treat cancer. Clinical
trials supported by the Campaign deliver promising new treatments to
the patient at the earliest possible opportunity and the charity
contributes directly to improvements in the care and cure of
patients through the Cancer Research Campaign
clinical departments.

The profits from this publication will be used to continue
the work of the Campaign.

Acknowledgements

It has given me a great deal of pleasure to be able to compile this book of entertaining and delicious recipes. I would not have been able to do it without the participation of the most sought after and busiest people, all of whom have given their recipes willingly and so very graciously. My thanks go primarily to them.

The Cancer Research Campaign is enormously grateful to the wonderful work done on this book by Hugh Tollemache, his team at Beshara Press, and Annie Lennox and Piers Thorogood in particular. Their encouragement, help and generosity have been outstanding. It should be noted that this book has been printed with a minimal profit being made by Beshara Press, thereby contributing maximum benefit to the charity.

I would like to thank Valerie Barr of Scone, by Perth, for taking so much time and trouble over the cover illustration.

My thanks also go to Christopher Cassell and the pupils of the following schools who kindly donated the text illustrations: The Academy, Perth; St Columba's High School, Perth; Pitlochry High School; Wadhurst Primary School; Ysgol Gyfun Pantycelyn, Llandovery.

Belinda Pinckney

CONTENTS

Her Majesty The Queen

Suprêmes de Faisan Reine d'Or

(serves 4)

Ingredients:

2 pheasants (plucked and dressed)
1 lb fresh chestnuts (prepared and puréed)
1/3 gill claret
2 oz grated strong Cheddar cheese
1 lb wild mushrooms (cooked in butter)
2 tablespoons vegetable oil

1/6 gill whisky
1 egg
salt, pepper, nutmeg
1 pint pheasant stock
1/4 pint single cream
2 oz butter
chopped chervil

Method:

Carefully remove the four breasts from the carcasses and trim to shape. Mince the pheasant trimmings finely, combine with the chestnut purée and add an egg to bind and seasoning. Make an incision in each of the breasts and fill with the chestnut stuffing.

Shallow fry gently in hot vegetable oil and a little butter until cooked.

Remove the breasts from the pan and keep warm.

Deglaze the pan with the whisky and then add the claret and pheasant stock (which can be made from the carcasses), reduce to a coating consistency and add the cream. Adjust seasoning, pass sauce through a fine strainer into a small pot and garnish with chopped chervil. Place the prepared wild mushrooms on the service dish and place the cooked breasts on them. Coat with the sauce and sprinkle with grated cheese and small pieces of butter.

Glaze beneath the grill until golden, then serve.

Guinea fowl or chicken breasts can be used as an alternative to the pheasant.

John Taylor, The Lord Taylor of Warwick

Cancer does not discriminate. It can affect the young, old, male and female. It does not acknowledge geographical boundaries or material wealth. Relatives and friends of cancer victims share the suffering.

The fight against cancer must continue. This is why the Cancer Research Campaign deserves all the support we can give it.

Caribbean Cod Stew
(serves 4)

This stew is great with potatoes, yams or rice. My Mum, Enid, used to make it. Tasty, filling and warming in the winter months growing up as a child in Birmingham! I used to wash it down with warm carrot juice – again home made.

Preparation time: 15 minutes
Cooking time: 22-25 minutes
Freezing: not recommended

500–750g (1–1 1/2 lb) cod fillet, skinned and cut into 4 pieces
500g (1 lb) beefsteak tomatoes, skinned and chopped
1 clove garlic, crushed
2 teaspoons chopped thyme
2 tablespoons olive oil
2 teaspoons soy sauce
2 onions, sliced
salt and pepper to taste

1. Sprinkle the cod with salt and pepper and rub all over with the garlic. Set aside for 15 minutes.

2. Meanwhile, heat the oil in a large saucepan, add the onions and fry gently until softened. Add the tomatoes, thyme and soy sauce, bring to the boil, then partly cover and simmer for 10 minutes, until pulpy.

3. Add the fish, cover and cook for 12–15 minutes until tender. Serve with steamed potatoes or yams.

Lady Macdonald of Macdonald
Kinloch Lodge
Sleat
Isle of Skye

Mushroom, Cheese and Garlic Soufflé
(serves 4–5)

3 oz (75 g) butter
1 onion, peeled and finely chopped
1 clove of garlic, peeled and finely chopped
4 oz (125 g) mushrooms, finely chopped
3 oz (75 g) plain flour
3/4 pint (425 ml) milk
6 large eggs
salt and freshly ground black pepper
a pinch of ground nutmeg
4 oz (125 g) mature Lancashire or Cheddar cheese, grated
extra butter for greasing
grated Parmesan cheese, optional

Butter a soufflé dish about 7 in (18 cm) in diameter, and dust with Parmesan cheese if you have some.

Melt the 3 oz (75 g) butter in a saucepan, add the chopped onion and garlic and cook gently for 7–10 minutes until the onion is soft and transparent. Add the finely chopped mushrooms and cook for about 1 minute, then stir in the flour. Gradually add the milk, stirring all the time until the sauce boils. Take the saucepan off the heat and leave to cool. Then separate the eggs, putting the whites in a clean bowl and beating the yolks one by one into the cooled sauce. You can prepare the soufflé to this stage in the morning, ready for supper that evening if you wish.

About three-quarters of an hour before you want to eat, whisk the egg whites until they are stiff, and, using a metal spoon, fold them quickly and thoroughly into the sauce. Pour this into the prepared soufflé dish and bake in a hot oven, 220°C / 425°F / gas mark 7 / the top right hand oven in a 4 door Aga. Bake for 40 minutes; if the diners are not quite ready another 5–10 minutes in the oven won't hurt.

Serve immediately – the soufflé will be soft in the centre. Serve with a green or tomato salad and with warm brown bread or rolls.

Mousseline of Scallops and Leek
with a Scallop Sauce
(serves 6)

For the mousseline:
1/2 lb fresh salmon (skinned and filleted)
    – buy a little extra to allow for wastage
1/2 lb fresh scallops
400 ml double cream
2 eggs (whole)
2 leeks (diced small and washed)
2 oz salted butter
salt and pepper
1 packet of crispy seaweed
    (from local Chinese take-away)

For the scallop sauce:
1/2 lb fresh scallops (demuscled and
    washed to remove any grit)
1 onion
1 bunch of tarragon
1/2 pint milk
1 pint chicken or fish stock
bay leaf
thickening granules
3 oz salted butter

Remove muscle and coral from scallops and set aside for sauce. Wash scallops to remove any grit.

Mousseline:
Sauté leeks in 2 oz butter until slightly soft but still green. Keep warm.
Butter 6 terrine moulds well and refrigerate.
Into Magimix put 1/2 lb salmon, 1/2 lb scallops, cream, eggs, and a little salt and pepper. Whiz until the mixture starts to become sloppy in texture. Pour into bowl and add sautéed warm leeks. Mix well and pour into buttered moulds – fill almost to the top. Put into a deep baking tray with a little water one-third of the way up the moulds and cook for about 20 minutes at 160°C or until firm to touch. Remove from oven and after leaving to rest for a while, turn out onto fresh mangetout or asparagus on plate and serve warm or hot with scallop sauce and crispy seaweed.

Scallop sauce:
Season trimmings of scallops and sauté in 3 oz salted butter. Put lid on. Let the scallops release their juices. Add prawn shell trimmings if you can get them from the fishmonger. Keeping lid on, sweat for a couple of minutes but don't let scallop liquid dry up.
Add 1 onion, roughly chopped, and some fresh tarragon.
Add 1/2 pint of milk (approximately 250 ml).
Add 1 pint of chicken or fish stock (approximately 500 ml) and bay leaf.
Bring to boil and *simmer* for 20 minutes, then strain.
Thicken with thickening granules (MacDougalls – available from all major supermarkets). Don't overdo them as they can become too glutinous but they will help cooks with very little time.
Add some chopped tarragon and pour over terrines.

The success of this quick sauce is to allow the fish juices to mix with the butter before adding the liquids. Do not boil fiercely.

Creole Chicken

(serves 4)

4 boneless, skinless chicken breasts
1 can of condensed tomato soup
1 onion
1 red / green pepper
250g / 8 oz mushrooms
1 tablespoon of olive oil
1 clove of garlic
1/2 teaspoon cayenne pepper
salt and pepper

Cut the chicken into thick slices and chop all the vegetables. Heat the olive oil in a wok or large frying-pan, add the chopped garlic, cayenne pepper and chicken, and stir fry on a high heat for 4–5 minutes. Add the onion, pepper and mushrooms and fry for a further 3 minutes. Pour in the can of condensed soup and half a can of water and stir all the ingredients together. Turn the heat down and simmer for 8–10 minutes, adding a pinch of salt and coarse ground black pepper to taste. Serve immediately with rice and crusty bread.

Dame Judi Dench

This is one of my favourite recipes – very quick and easy for anyone leading a hectic life!

Poached Salmon

Clean the fish, then squeeze over it fresh lemon juice and a good quantity of freshly ground black pepper. Wrap in foil.

Bring a fish kettle of water to the boil, add the fish, and continue boiling for two minutes only. Remove the pan from the heat and leave in a cool place. When the water is hand-hot, the fish will be cooked. Serve with the sauce of your choice.

This method works for any size fish.

John le Carré

Recipe for Cancer Research Campaign's Celebrity Cook Book

Take
one consenting adult
one fat wallet
and one taxi

to the Connaught in Carlos Place, London W1, together with a good appetite, an inexhaustible delight in tipping whatever moves, never mind if you tip the occasional guest by mistake in your enthusiasm.

Abandon
all sense of shame for a good three hours.

Eat
everything your nanny told you to, and your doctor told you not to: quails' eggs with a mornay sauce in little pastry boats and calories whirling round them like flies; steak and kidney pie with roast potatoes that should be arrested on sight for corrupting the over-age; then for the main, main course the outrageous bread and butter pudding, which every good cook thinks he or she can pop home and reproduce but can't – it's some low secret that no spy has yet been able to steal.

Then, in remorse and gratitude, send a fat cheque to Cancer Research Campaign.

David Wilson
The Peat Inn
Fife

Braised Venison Shanks with Flageolet Beans
(serves 8)

8 venison shanks
600g carrots
600g celery
1/2 pt dry white wine
6 cloves garlic
6 juniper berries
bouquet garni (chervil, thyme,
   rosemary, tarragon, bayleaf)

600g onions
olive oil for frying
1200g tinned tomatoes
50g unsalted butter
salt and pepper
venison stock

1. Chop vegetables.
2. Heat oil in pan, brown shanks on all sides.
3. Transfer to stock pot.
4. Brown vegetables in pan then add white wine to deglaze. Add to stock pot.
5. Add tomatoes and crushed garlic, then cover with half venison stock/half water.
6. Add bouquet garni and simmer for about 2–3 hours until meat is very tender.
7. Remove shanks and keep warm.
8. Strain all the cooking liquid through sieve pushing vegetables through to extract all the juices and flavours.
9. Return to heat and reduce until thick enough to coat back of spoon. Whisk in butter, in small pieces. Check seasoning.

Flageolet Beans

2 1/2 cups flageolet beans
200g chopped carrot
200g chopped turnip
2 cloves garlic
salt and pepper
2 1/2 pt chicken stock or light
   game stock

200g chopped onion
200g chopped celery
150g butter
1 bunch thyme
parsley or chervil, chopped

1. Soak beans overnight in cold water.
2. In a large pan melt half (75g) butter, add diced vegetables with 4 tbsp water, cook over a low heat for about 25 minutes until soft but not coloured.
3. Add crushed garlic cloves and beans. Stir to mix. Pour in stock, add thyme, leave to cook for about 1 1/2 hours. Beans should be soft to the bite and juices quite thick.
4. Season and stir in remaining butter.

To serve: Spoon flageolet beans on to warm plate. Place venison shank in centre of plate then coat with reduced sauce. Sprinkle chopped parsley or chervil over beans.

Girl Friday's Lime Rice
by Joanna Lumley

For 4 generous servings.

Put 2 mugs of Basmati rice into boiling water which is flavoured with a vegetable stock cube. One large saucepan should have a whole cube — if you have 4 cardamums toss them in as well. Boil rice until cooked ie. till there is a pinprick of white in the centre of a bitten grain. Drain, put in covered serve sieve over an inch of practically boiling water for 3 mins to steam dry ——— then serve as an accompaniment to vegetable curry, drenched in the juice of four lovely ripe limes

Sir Colin Davis

A Fast and Easy Supper
for 4–6 People

Starter
lettuce leaves, any variety washed and spun
walnuts, chopped
100 g / 4 oz Roquefort cheese, finely grated
a few rashers of smoked streaky bacon, fried until crispy then chopped
walnut or olive oil

Assemble the lettuce, walnuts and bacon in a large salad bowl. Add the oil and toss. Serve on individual plates and garnish with the grated Roquefort cheese.

Main dish – Duck with Almonds
500 g / 1 lb lean duck meat (or fillet of pork, rump steak or chicken breast)
2 slices of root ginger, shredded
1 clove of garlic, crushed
3 tablespoons olive oil
4 spring onions
100 g / 4 oz mangetout
100 g / 4 oz mushrooms
2 tablespoons sherry
2 teaspoons cornflour
3 tablespoons soy sauce
flaked almonds, toasted

Slice the meat and place in a bowl with the ginger and garlic. Pour over 1 tablespoon of oil and marinate for 30 minutes.

Slice the mushrooms and spring onions.

Heat the remaining oil in a deep frying pan. Add the spring onions and the meat and cook for 3 minutes. Add the mushrooms and mangetout and cook for another 2 minutes. Add the sherry and soy sauce.

Blend the cornflour with a tablespoon of water and stir into the pan.
Cook for 1 more minute until thickened.

Stir in the toasted almonds and serve with rice or potatoes.

Sir Colin Davis's *Fast and Easy Supper continued*

Dessert – Summer Fruit

"The cleverest thing I ever did" said the White Knight to Alice "was inventing a new pudding during the meat course".

1 banana per person
75–125g / 3–5 oz brown sugar
2–4 tablespoons lemon juice
50g / 2 oz butter
3 tablespoons brandy

Slice the bananas in half length-ways and fry for a few minutes in the butter. Sprinkle with the brown sugar and lemon juice and cook for another 2 minutes. Pour brandy over them and serve, flaming!

Frankie Dettori

One Meal a Day

Go to the fish shop and buy any piece of fish you want. Steam the fish and serve with a small salad or vegetables!

Christopher McHardy

11

Dame Barbara Cartland

Salmon is one of the richest fish that exists. The continued belief since Roman times that oysters, fish, especially salmon, raw eggs, raw vegetables, pomegranates and honey lead to increased sexual prowess is right.

Salmon Coulibiac
(serves 4)

I have seen this dish cooked so often on television but I think the way my Chef does it makes the salmon more moist and appetising.

Chef – Nigel Gordon

Ingredients:

1/2 lb puff pastry	1/4 pint cream
1/2 lb fresh salmon (cooked)	1/2 lb homemade mayonnaise
2 eggs (hard boiled)	1 onion (chopped)
1/2 lb mushrooms (sliced)	egg yolk, for glazing

Make the pastry and chill for 1 hour. Meanwhile pound the salmon and mix with half the mayonnaise.

Separate the egg whites from the yolks and chop finely. Sauté the onion until soft, add the mushrooms and continue cooking for 5 minutes.

Roll out the pastry into a rectangle and arrange the ingredients for the filling in layers, with the salmon on the bottom, the mushrooms and onion next, and finally the egg yolks and whites on top.

Close up the pastry, folding over the edges from each side. Shape the coulibiac so that it resembles a fish, decorate with small round pieces of pastry-like scales and brush over with egg yolk.

Bake in a hot oven – 400°F, Mark 6, for 3/4 of an hour.

Add cream to the remaining mayonnaise and serve separately.

Rowan Atkinson

Mr. Bean Recipe
Baked Beans on Toast

Heat the beans in a pan until they go all bubbly.

Pour over toast and serve.

Susan King

Sir Hardy Amies
(This recipe was kindly sent by Sir Hardy's cook, Mrs. P.M. Mildenhall, on his behalf.)

Lamb Cutlets in Apricot Sauce
(serves 4)

1/2 onion, peeled	3 oz (no soak) dried apricots
1/2 oz butter	1 tbsp cooking oil
8 lamb cutlets	1/2 tsp ground cinnamon
1/4 pt lamb stock	salt and pepper

1. Thinly slice the onion and cut the apricots into slivers.
2. Heat the butter and oil in a heavy-based frying pan. Add the lamb cutlets and brown on both sides. Remove and set aside.
3. Add the onion to the pan and cook until softened. Stir in the apricots and cinnamon. Return the lamb cutlets to the pan and pour over the stock. Season and bring to the boil. Cover and simmer gently for 15 minutes, or until the meat is tender.
4. Transfer the cutlets to a warmed serving dish and pour the sauce over them.

This dish can be served with new potatoes, green salad, sugar snap peas or green beans. It is not suitable for freezing.

Thomas Allen

Wholewheat Bread

This is a recipe I make on a very regular basis and it includes my secret special ingredients – specially given for Cancer Research Campaign. It is my own tried and trusted variation on a well-known recipe.

2–3 tsp brown sugar
4 tsp dried yeast
4 tsp salt

1 pt + 6 fl oz hand-hot water
1 kg bag of malted brown flour
pistachio nuts, walnuts,
    caraway seeds

To a measuring jug add 6 fl oz of "uncomfortable to the hand" hot water (any cooler the yeast won't work). Add 2–3 tsp brown sugar and 4 tsp yeast. Stir once or twice and set aside to ferment.

Add 1 kg of flour to a large mixing bowl. Ideally the flour should be warm.

Add to flour 4 tsp of salt and the nuts and caraway. I add a couple of tsp of brown sugar usually too. Mix them together with the hand – very therapeutic!

When the fermentation has taken place there should be a head on the yeast mixture, doubling the volume (i.e. 12 fl oz).

Make a crater in the flour and slowly add the yeast mixture, stirring it in each time until wholly absorbed. When complete, fill the measuring jug with a pint of water of similar temperature and gradually add this, mixing all the time.

When it is of a still slightly sticky consistency it should be right.

Cut into two halves and put these into two buttered loaf tins. Set aside for half an hour in a warm place covered with a damp cloth to prove.

Set the oven at 180°C and bake when the dough has risen slightly.

Baking time, 30–35 minutes.

Tip out of the tin and give them 5 minutes more.

Eat immediately with lots of butter and honey or strawberry jam.

The Rt. Hon. Paddy Ashdown, M.P.

Pasta with Two Cheeses

This is one of the family's favourite supper dishes. You can vary the amounts according to how many you have to feed. This recipe is for two people.

1 large tin (15 oz / 375 g) plum tomatoes
1 clove garlic, chopped
1 tbsp of olive oil (any oil will do)
2 tsp of dried basil or 5 fresh
  basil leaves

2 oz / 50 g mature Cheddar cheese, grated
5 oz / 125 g packet of Mozzarella cheese,
  chopped into cubes
Any sort of pasta!

The Rt. Hon. Paddy Ashdown, M.P.'s *Pasta with Two Cheeses continued*

Put a large pan of lightly salted water on to boil.

In a heavy-based pan, mash the tomatoes with the back of a wooden spoon, add the oil, basil and garlic, and simmer gently so that the sauce thickens.

When the water boils, add the pasta, following the cooking instructions on the pack. It normally takes 10 minutes for pasta to be ready.

Now add the two cheeses to the tomato sauce, turning the heat right down. Stir well once, then leave while the pasta finishes off. If the sauce starts to stick, turn off the heat and cover with a lid to keep it hot.

Once the pasta is cooked, drain well, place the tomato and cheese sauce on top and serve immediately with a crisp green salad.

Jane Asher

Minty Lamb Risotto
(serves 4)

Preparation time: approximately 30 minutes

250 g (8 oz) lean lamb fillet, finely diced
1 onion, diced
1 green pepper, diced
1 large courgette, diced
250 g (8 oz) risotto rice
450 ml (3/4 pint) lamb stock
425 g (14oz) can chopped tomatoes
2 tablespoons freshly chopped mint
salt and freshly ground black pepper
sprigs of fresh mint to garnish

Fry the lamb in a saucepan without any oil, add the onion and pepper. Cook gently for 6–8 minutes, stirring occasionally.

Add the courgette and rice, then stir in the stock, chopped tomatoes, mint and seasoning to taste.

Bring to the boil and simmer gently for 15 minutes or until the rice is tender and the liquid has been absorbed.

Transfer to a warmed serving plate and garnish with the fresh mint. Serve with a tomato and onion salad.

Lord Archer

Creamed Seafood Bake

(serves 4–6)

For the rice:
long grain brown rice measured to 10 fl oz in a glass measuring jug
1 pint boiling water
1/2 onion, finely chopped
1 tsp oil
3 oz raisins

For the seafood sauce:
1 1/2 lb mixed seafood, such as prawns,
  halibut, scallops – sliced/chunks
4 oz mushrooms, sliced
4 oz butter
2 tsp fresh root ginger, peeled and grated
2 tsp hot curry powder
3 fl oz dry sherry
1 oz plain flour
1/2 tsp mustard powder
1/2 pt single cream
4 oz Cheddar cheese, grated
pinch cayenne pepper
salt and black pepper

Set oven to 400°F (200°C, Gas Mark 6).
Have ready a baking dish, 8 in x 12 in.

Lightly fry rice and onion for 5 minutes and add raisins. Pour on water, bring to the boil, simmer for 40 minutes until the rice is tender.

Meanwhile, melt 2 oz butter, fry mushrooms for 2–3 minutes, then remove from pan. Add another 1 oz butter to the pan and then add seafood and sherry.

Cook for 4–5 minutes then add to the mushrooms.

Pour remaining juices in the pan into a jug and add last ounce of butter to the pan. Add flour, ginger, curry powder and mustard and gradually stir in the reserved fish juices. Stir and cook until thickened. Pour this sauce over fish and mushrooms.

Arrange the rice in the base of the baking dish. Spoon the fish mixture over, sprinkle with cheese and a dusting of cayenne pepper and bake for 30 minutes.

Mohamed Al Fayed
Chairman of Harrods and L'Hotel Ritz, Paris

Ritzy Beef

Ingredients:
4 fillet mignons, cut 1" thick
salt and freshly ground black
    pepper
4 tablespoons butter
1 shallot, finely chopped
2 cups fresh mushrooms, quartered
1/2 cup beef stock
1/2 cup Madeira, or additional beef stock
chopped parsley for garnish, optional

Method:
Season the beef with salt and pepper then, in a medium sauté pan, melt 2 tablespoons of the butter. When the butter stops foaming, sauté the fillets for 6–7 minutes on each side, for a medium rare steak. Remove the meat from the pan and pour off any grease.

In a small sauté pan, melt the remaining butter. Sauté the shallot for 2 minutes. Add the mushrooms and cook for 3 minutes until lightly browned. Set aside.

In the meat pan, add the stock and boil rapidly, scraping the pan, until 2 tablespoons of liquid remain. Add the Madeira and boil rapidly until the sauce thickens, approximately 2–3 minutes. Put the mushroom mixture back in and simmer for a minute more. Serve the steaks with the sauce over the top and garnish with parsley if desired.

This recipe can be carried off with great aplomb by the home cook who knows his or her onions, or should I say shallots?

Vladimir Ashkenazy

Beef Casserole
(serves 4)

800 g stewing beef (lean, cut into pieces)
300 g mushrooms (thickly sliced)
4 carrots (thickly sliced)
2 medium onions (skinned and sliced)
1 small tin tomato purée
100 ml red wine
900 ml beef stock
3 tbs flour
50 gm butter
salt and pepper

Angela Piper

1. Coat beef pieces in flour seasoned with salt and pepper. Heat butter in pan and brown beef pieces. Remove from pan and place in ovenproof casserole.
2. Add the sliced carrots.
3. Brown onions and mushrooms in pan (add more butter if required) and fry for approximately 5 minutes until lightly brown. Stir in remaining flour, beef stock, red wine and tomato purée.
4. Pour over meat and carrots. Cover and place in moderate oven (150°C, 300°F) for 2 1/2 hours. Serve with boiled potatoes.

Sir Alan Ayckbourn

Fish Dish
(for 12 people)

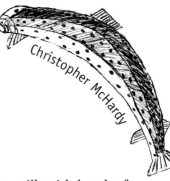

Christopher McHardy

1 lb salmon	3 lb (approx) fillets of haddock
4 oz gruyère cheese	10 oz crème fraîche
2 lb potatoes	2 oz flour
1/2 lb peeled prawns	2 oz butter
2 bunches of watercress	bay leaf
1 pt milk	fresh prawns to decorate

Poach salmon and haddock (can use frozen) in 1/2 pint of the milk with bay leaf. When cooked, flake fish and put in dish.
Make a sauce (a roux with the butter and flour, adding the milk the fish has been cooked in plus the remaining 1/2 pint); then add the gruyère cheese and crème fraîche.
Peel and cook potatoes then cut into cubes.
Cover cooked fish with chopped watercress, then cheese sauce, then potatoes, and cook uncovered in oven (gas Mark 6) for half an hour.
Decorate the finished dish with a few fresh prawns.

The Rt. Hon. Gillian Shephard, M.P.

Cheese and Onion Pie

6 oz (175 g) shortcrust pastry
2 medium sized parboiled onions
1 tbsp seasoned flour
3–4 oz (75–110 g) grated Cheddar cheese
2 tbsp milk

Divide pastry and roll out two thirds to cover heatproof plate or dish. Slice onions finely, dip in seasoned flour, place on pastry and add cheese and milk. Cover pie with rest of pastry cut into strips and worked lattice fashion over the top.

Bake in a moderately hot oven 425°F or gas mark 7 for about 45 minutes until onion is tender.

Peter Alliss

The Story of the Pike

I am sending you a spoof recipe which was given to me years ago by my dear friend Peter Cook. We were talking about recipes whilst at the Gleneagles Hotel, which is one of my favourite watering holes, and he said to me "Have you ever tasted Pike?" and I said "As far as I know it's inedible". "Oh no no", he said. "A good sized 20 lb Pike can be beautiful. Top and tail it and clean it out, then you get two pieces of hickory board and you place it on the hickory board. You then cover it with a generous amount of butter, some herbs sprinkled on the top and you place the other piece of hickory on top of the fish and tie or wire it together. Put it in a fish kettle, add a bottle of Bollinger Vintage Champagne, a bottle of Cointreau, half a pint of fresh orange juice, some sliced, fresh peaches, half a pint of Drambuie and a pint of sparkling water. Allow to simmer gently, making sure you don't lose any of the sauce. Throw it immediately into a dustbin, get your best Waterford crystal out of the cupboard and enjoy the gravy."

Michael Barrymore

Beef Wellington
(serves 4–6)

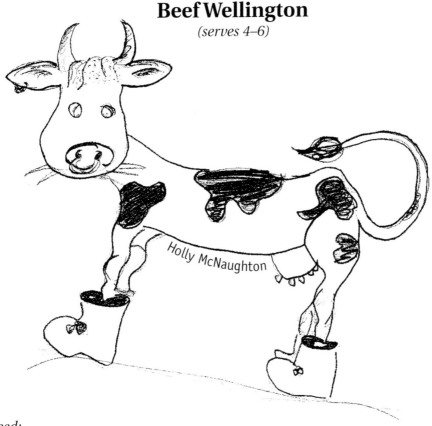

Holly McNaughton

You need:

8 oz puff pastry
2 lb fillet steak
3 oz butter
salt and pepper

8 oz mushrooms, finely chopped
2 small onions, finely chopped
1 tablespoon chopped parsley

Glaze: 1 egg, 1 tablespoon of water

Oven: 220°C / 425°F or Gas Mark 7

What you do:
Spread the steak with half the butter, roast as beef, but slightly undercook. Allow to cool. Blend mushrooms and onions with remaining butter, parsley and salt.

Roll pastry until very thin oblong shape, large enough to envelop meat. Spread onion mixture, leaving a border of 1/2 inch. Place steak in the centre, moisten edges with a little water, and fold to cover meat. Seal the ends and the join and turn so that this is underneath. Put onto a baking tray. Make two or three slits in the pastry to allow steam to escape. Beat the egg with the water and brush over pastry. Bake in the centre of a hot oven for 35–40 minutes.

Raymond Blanc

All-Bran Tuiles
Layered with Raspberries and Bio Yoghurt
(serves 4)

Planning ahead: The tuile mixture may be made a day in advance and the tuiles themselves 6 or so hours then stored in an airtight container.

Ingredients

The tuiles
35g Kellogg's All-Bran
35g sesame seeds
75g icing sugar
25g chick pea flour
50g melted unsalted butter
zest and juice of 1 orange

The raspberries and yoghurt
4 punnets of ripe raspberries
sugar to taste
120g bio yoghurt
1 tbsp sugar

Method: Preheat your oven to 190°C

The tuiles
Mix all of the dry ingredients together then stir in the butter, orange zest and juice.

To cook the tuiles you need to do 3 batches, the mixture will make about 20 and you only require 12, so the spoils go to the chef!

Place 10g (approx. 1 dessertspoonful) of the mixture onto a non-stick tray, allowing enough space in between them so that they can spread to about 8 cm diameter. Then flatten them with the back of a fork dipped into a little water. Bake in the preheated oven for about 8 minutes until golden brown. Remove from the oven and allow to cool and set slightly, then transfer the tuiles to a cooling rack with a palette knife. Reserve until needed.

The raspberries and yoghurt
Purée 2 punnets of the raspberries and sweeten to taste with the sugar. Strain through a fine sieve to remove the seeds then set aside. Mix the bio yoghurt with the sugar and set aside.

Finishing the dish and serving
Spoon the raspberry purée around the bases of four plates. Top with a tuile then alternate with the bio yoghurt and remaining raspberries finishing with a tuile on top.

Decorate with a dollop of yoghurt and raspberries and a mint sprig.

David Gower

Beef Wellington with Pâté

(serves 6–8)

3 lb beef fillet
1/4 lb pâté
1/2 lb finely chopped mushrooms
1 lb puff pastry (or shortcrust)
beaten egg to glaze
salt, pepper and 1 tbsp oil

Pre-heat oven to 220°C/425°F.
Rub the beef with salt, pepper and oil.
Roast on a rack for 40 minutes.
Remove and leave to cool.

When cool, cover the top and sides with pâté
and chopped mushrooms.

Roll out the pastry to 1/4" thick – large enough
to envelop the meat.
Put the fillet top side down on the pastry, and
enclose into a parcel, sealing the ends.
Turn meat seam side down and decorate with
spare pastry if you can be bothered!
Glaze with the beaten egg.

Bake for a further 40 minutes or so, till the
pastry is golden brown and puffed up.

Tastes even better if served with a red
wine sauce.

Gemma Cameron

Dennis Taylor

Rebecca Gilmour
aged 8

Toulouse Cassoulet
(serves 5)

1 thyme sprig
2 bay leaves
100 g/3 1/2 oz butter
1 can tomato purée
2 tbsp Armagnac
1 Toulouse sausage
60 g/2 oz breadcrumbs
salt and freshly ground black pepper
500 g/1 lb 2 oz salt pork belly (diced)
1 kg/2 1/4 lb boned shoulder of lamb
500 g/ 1 lb 2 oz dried haricot beans (soaked overnight and drained)

Gemma Duncan

Pre-heat oven at 200°C
/ 400°F / gas mark 6. Place beans in casserole dish, add thyme and bay leaves, arrange pork on top and fill with enough cold water to cover. Put on lid and cook for 15 minutes. Reduce temperature to 180°C / 350°F / gas mark 4. Continue cooking for 2 1/2 hours. Add water if necessary.

Dennis Taylor's *Toulouse Cassoulet continued*

Cut lamb into 10 pieces, melt half of the butter in the frying pan and sauté lamb pieces for 30 minutes, add to beans and pork and stir in tomato purée and Armagnac. Season and return to oven for 30 minutes. Meanwhile, cut sausage into 5 pieces and fry in remainder of butter for 10 minutes. Remove casserole dish from oven and increase temperature to 220°C / 425°F / gas mark 7.

Place sausage on top of bean mixture and sprinkle with half of the breadcrumbs. Return to oven uncovered for 15 minutes. Remove again and stir well. Sprinkle remainder of the breadcrumbs and cook for 15 minutes. Serve very hot.

Viscount and Viscountess Younger of Leckie

Mustard and Sugar Pork Chops

(serves 4)

Ingredients:
4 lean pork chops
Meaux/wholegrain mustard
demerara sugar
salt and pepper

Method:
Line a roasting tin with foil.
Spread mustard on the top of the chops and
sprinkle on the demerara sugar.
Put in a roasting oven for about 20–30 minutes
until the tops are brown and crispy.
Remove the chops.
Add water to the foil-lined cooking tin,
allowing the brown bits on the foil to mix with the
water and make gravy.
Season to taste.
Pour the gravy over and serve.

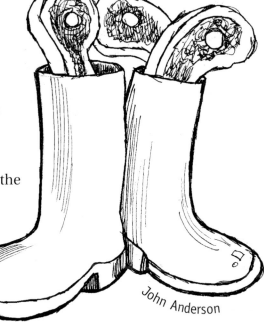

John Anderson

Raymond Blanc
Le Manoir aux Quat' Saisons
Great Milton, Oxford

Fricassée de Volaille au Vinaigre et Estragon
(Chicken fricassée with vinegar and tarragon)
(for 4 people)

Planning ahead: *Ask your butcher to cut the bird into eight pieces plus the two wings, off the backbone, and also to remove the wish bone. You will also need 300g (11 oz) chicken bones, finely chopped, for the stock. The stock can be prepared 1 day in advance, and the fricassée half an hour before the meal (it should be kept warm).*

1 roasting chicken, about 1.4kg (3 lb) in weight,
    cut into 10 pieces, including the 2 wings
15g (1/2 oz) unsalted butter
salt and freshly ground pepper

1 tbsp corn oil
50ml (2 fl oz) white wine vinegar

For the stock:
chopped backbones from the chicken, plus
    300g (11oz) of other chicken bones
10g (1/4 oz) unsalted butter
1 tbsp corn oil
1/2 small onion, peeled and chopped
1 garlic clove, peeled and crushed
120ml (4 fl oz) dry white wine
4 ripe medium tomatoes, chopped, leaving the seeds in
1 tsp tomato purée
1 sprig of thyme
2 sprigs of tarragon

For the sauce:
1 tsp Dijon mustard
40g (1 1/2 oz) cold unsalted butter, diced
1 level tbsp very finely chopped chives

1 tbsp whipping cream
1 level tbsp chopped tarragon

Preparing the stock: In a large saucepan, sear and lightly colour the chopped chicken bones in the butter and oil for 10 minutes. Add the chopped onion and garlic and sweat for a further 2–3 minutes. Add the white wine and boil to reduce by one-third. Add the chopped tomato and the tomato purée, thyme and tarragon, and cover with water. Bring to the boil, skim and simmer the stock for 20 minutes. Pass through a fine sieve, pressing down with the back of a spoon to extract as much liquid as possible. Cool and then refrigerate. You should have about 200ml (7 fl oz).
Preheat the oven to 400°F (200°C) Gas 6.

Raymond Blanc's *Fricassée de Volaille continued*

Cooking the fricassée: In a large cast-iron casserole, heat the butter and oil, and sear the chicken pieces, skin side down, turning them over after 2 minutes. Season with salt and pepper, cover and place in the preheated oven for 25 minutes, leaving the lid slightly ajar. Remove from the oven. Turn the oven down to 325°F (160°C) Gas 3.

Place the casserole on the top of the cooker and spoon out as much fat as possible. Add the vinegar, bring to the boil, and reduce the vinegar until it has totally evaporated. Turn the chicken pieces as you boil, until they are nicely coloured. Arrange the chicken pieces on a flat serving dish and keep warm in the low oven.

Making the sauce: Add the mustard to the casserole and gradually whisk in the 200ml (7 fl oz) stock, scraping the caramelised juices off the bottom. Strain into a saucepan, then add the cream. Whisk in the cold diced butter, then finally add the tarragon and chives.

Serving: Remove the chicken pieces from the oven, pour the sauce over them and serve to your guests.

Chef's note: The best way to remove the fat is to refrigerate the stock; the fat will solidify on the top and then it is easy to remove. This fat can be kept and used for pastry or roasting.

© *Cooking For Friends* published by Hodder Headline

Julie Friend
Masterchef 1997
These two recipes which Julie kindly sent us led to her win on Masterchef.

Potato and Parsnip Cakes
(makes 4)

2 medium red skinned potatoes, grated
4 small parsnips, cored and grated
1 egg yolk, beaten
olive oil for frying and greasing
salt and freshly ground black pepper

Place the grated vegetables into a clean tea towel and wring to squeeze out all the excess liquid. DO NOT RINSE.
In a bowl mix the grated potato and parsnip with the beaten egg yolk and season with salt and pepper.
Drizzle a thin film of olive oil into a heavy-based frying pan and heat to hot. Divide the potato mixture into four and shape into rounds. Press down with a fish slice and re-shape. The cakes should be about 1 cm thick.
Fry for about 5 minutes or until the underside is golden brown and then turn and fry the other side. Remove from the pan and drain on kitchen paper.

Julie Friend
Masterchef 1997

Rosemary Lamb with Redcurrant Sauce
(serves 4)

a few black peppercorns
2 tsp dried rosemary
2 racks of lamb, each with at least 6 cutlets, trimmed of all fat
300 ml / 1/2 pint fruity red wine such as Shiraz or Merlot
1 red onion, thinly sliced
1 carrot, chopped
1 tbsp redcurrant jelly
2 tbsps olive oil
knob of butter
salt and freshly ground black pepper
sprigs of rosemary to garnish

Method:
Using a pestle and mortar, crush together the peppercorns and dried rosemary then rub over the lamb. Place in a non-metallic dish and cover with three quarters of the wine. Add the onion and carrot and leave for about 1 hour.

Preheat the oven to 200C/Gas 6/400F. Remove the lamb from the dish. Strain the marinade into a bowl and keep to one side. Reserve the vegetables.

Heat the oil in a frying pan. Cut the racks in half and sear each side for about 1 minute. Transfer to a roasting tin. Reserve the pan with its juices.

Roast the lamb for about 12 minutes for medium rare or longer if preferred. Once cooked to your liking remove from the oven, cover with foil and leave to rest for about 10 minutes.

Reheat the reserved frying juices. Add the reserved vegetables and fry until coloured. Stir in the remaining wine and allow to bubble until almost evaporated. Remove the vegetables and discard. Pour the reserved marinade into the pan and boil rapidly until the sauce begins to thicken and become syrupy. Stir in the redcurrant jelly, and knob of butter, and season to taste with salt and pepper.

Slice the lamb cutlets and serve on a potato and parsnip cake (see previous page). Spoon the sauce over the lamb and garnish with a little rosemary.

The Rt. Hon. Betty Boothroyd, M.P.
Madam Speaker

Stewed Oxtail
(serves 4)

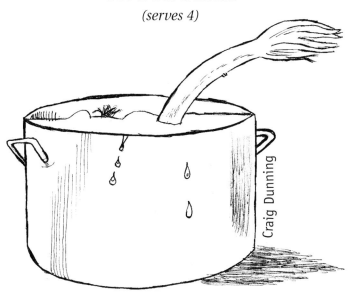

Craig Dunning

Ingredients:

1 oxtail divided at the joints	3 carrots, diced
1 large onion, sliced	3–4 young turnips, diced
1 tablespoon lemon juice	

Optional ingredients:

3 cloves	1 blade of mace
1/4 teaspoon allspice	bouquet garni
seasoning	

Method:
Place oxtail in saucepan and cover with water. Boil for 1/4 hour.
Drain to remove scum.
Replace meat in pan, add vegetables, seasoning and spices and herbs if used.
Cover with fresh water.
Simmer until tender – approximately 2 1/2 hours.
Add lemon juice.
Serve on a hot dish with croûtons or snippets of toast.

Oxtail takes a long time to cook so it is well to cook it partially the day before. Another advantage of this is that it can be set in a bowl overnight, the grease will be solidified on top by the next morning and can then be skimmed off. This makes the stew less rich and much more digestible.

Cilla Black

Chinese Style Steak

fillet of sirloin steak
butter and oil
mushrooms
soy sauce
black peppercorns
cream

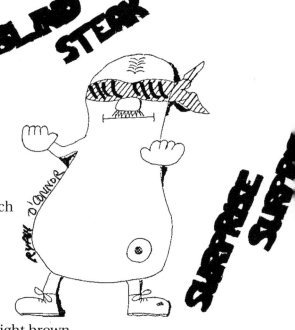

Crush the black peppercorns in a pestle and mortar and press them into the steak. Leave for at least 20 minutes to allow the flavour to penetrate.
Melt some butter in a frying pan (add a touch of oil to stop the butter burning) and add the steaks. Throw in some finely sliced mushrooms and stir them round the steak while it cooks.
When the steak is ready, add some cream and enough soy sauce to colour, until both the colour and taste is right. It should be a light brown.
Serve the steak with the sauce and garnish with vegetables or a salad.

The Rt. Hon. Ken Livingstone, M.P.

Spaghetti alla Trapanese

2 dessertspoons of pesto
8 large ripe tomatoes, peeled and chopped
1/2 teaspoon dried red chilli
salt and pepper
1 lb dried spaghetti
4 medium potatoes, boiled, peeled and diced
2 tablespoons virgin olive oil
4 tablespoons grated Parmesan, plus extra to serve

Mix tomatoes, pesto, chilli in a bowl. Add salt and pepper. Cook potatoes and dice. While spaghetti is cooking, toss the potatoes in the olive oil and place on a baking sheet. Place under a preheated grill until potatoes are golden. Drain pasta and place in serving dish. Add raw tomato sauce and hot potatoes. Toss well.
Sprinkle with grated Parmesan. Serve with extra Parmesan and with a green salad.

With acknowledgement to Viana La Place – Vegetables Italian Style

Darcey Bussell

Tagliatelle Primavera
(for 2)

8 oz tagliatelle
asparagus
grated Parmesan
crème fraîche
salt, pepper, olive oil
fresh herbs as available, chopped
fresh peas, if available
young broad beans, if available
(Substitute other vegetables for peas
and/or beans if necessary – maybe broccoli
or fennel if they are in season.)
onions and/or garlic to taste.

Quantities of vegetables can
be varied depending on what
is available and degree of
hunger.

Cook all vegetables except
onion until verging on
tender but still slightly
crispy. Cut into even-sized
pieces.

Michelle Quinn

Cook pasta as usual, and at the same
time fry the onion and/or garlic until soft in a
little olive oil. Once the onion is ready, add the other vegetables to heat through and
then keep warm.

As soon as the pasta is done, drain it and add a little oil (just to stop it sticking), salt,
pepper, herbs and Parmesan. Toss thoroughly to combine and add the vegetables and
crème fraîche to taste. Toss again. Transfer to a warmed serving dish and garnish with
a final sprinkle of Parmesan and herbs.

*Needless to say, this is a fairly classic dish so I am not claiming originality. I thought I
would send you a pasta recipe as the carbohydrate content is excellent for dancers when
we are working hard.*

31

Frances Bissell
The Times Cook

Roast Haunch of Wild Boar with gin,
blackcurrant liqueur, coriander and juniper,
on a bed of celeriac

Michael McMahon

Frances Bissell
The Times Cook

Roast Haunch of Wild Boar
with gin, blackcurrant liqueur,
coriander and juniper, on a bed of celeriac
(serves 8–10, plus leftovers)

1 haunch (leg) of wild boar
1 tablespoon juniper berries
1 tablespoon coriander seeds
1 tablespoon coarse sea salt
2 tablespoons English grain mustard
leaves of a good sprig of rosemary, snipped up
grated zest of 2 lemons, and the juice of 1
1 tablespoon freshly ground black pepper
150 ml Plymouth gin
4–5 tablespoons Devon blackcurrant liqueur
1 kg prepared celeriac

Have the boar skin removed in one piece. Trim off much of the fat and wipe the meat all over.

Grind the juniper berries, coriander and rosemary with the salt, and mix with the rest of the ingredients, apart from the celeriac. Rub the paste over the meat, cover with the skin, and leave for an hour or two, or overnight if more convenient.

Peel and trim the celeriac into cork-size pieces and arrange in a greased roasting dish. Place haunch on top, cover with the skin, and place in the oven. Cook for 25–30 minutes a pound at 150°C / 300°F / gas mark 2, plus, at the end, an extra 20 minutes at 200°C / 400° F / gas mark 6. Allow the meat to rest for 20 minutes before discarding the skin and carving the meat into thin slices.

Serve with extra root vegetables, roasted in the oven, steamed vegetables such as celery, leeks and fennel, and the celeriac made into a purée. Make a gravy with the boiled-down meat juices, and serve with a little homemade sharp fruit jelly as an accompaniment.

From *The Times Cook's Kitchen*
© Frances Bissell 1996

Gary Rhodes

Bread and Butter Pudding

(serves 6–8)

Bread and butter pudding has become one of our great classics. It was always a good way of using up stale bread with milk, sugar and eggs, but this would often result in a firm and tasteless pud, which left it with a bad name. This recipe will give you quite a different dish. I'm using just egg yolks and half milk and double cream, which is obviously a little more expensive to make, but once you've tried it you'll never want to make it any other way!

12 medium slices white bread	300 ml (10 fl oz) milk
50 g (2 oz) unsalted butter, softened	300 ml (10 fl oz) double cream
8 egg yolks	25 g (1 oz) sultanas
175 g (6 oz) caster sugar	25 g (1 oz) raisins
1 vanilla pod or a few drops of vanilla essence	

To finish: caster sugar

Method:
Grease a 1.75 litre (3 pint) pudding basin with butter.
Firstly, remove the crusts and butter the bread. Whisk the egg yolks and caster sugar together in a bowl. Split the vanilla pod and place in a pan with the milk and cream. Bring the milk and cream to the simmer, then sieve on to the egg yolks, stirring all the time. You now have the custard.

Arrange the bread in layers in the prepared basin, sprinkling the sultanas and raisins in between layers. Finish with a final layer of bread without any fruit on top as this tends to burn. The warm egg mixture may now be poured over the bread and cooked straightaway, but I prefer to pour the custard over the pudding then leave it to soak into the bread for 20 minutes before cooking. This allows the bread to take on a new texture and have the flavours all the way through.

Pre-heat the oven to 180°C / 350°F / gas mark 4.

Once the bread has been soaked, place the dish in a roasting tray three-quarters filled with warm water and place in the pre-heated oven. Cook for about 20–30 minutes in the pre-heated oven until the pudding begins to set. Because we are using only egg yolks, the mixture cooks like a fresh custard and only thickens; it should not become too firm.

When ready, remove from the water bath, sprinkle liberally with caster sugar to cover, and glaze under the grill on medium heat. The sugar should dissolve and caramelize and you may find that the corners of the bread start to burn a little. This helps the flavours, though, giving a bittersweet taste, and certainly looks good. The bread and butter pudding is now ready to serve and when you take that first spoonful and place it into a bowl you will see the custard just seeping from the dish – it's delicious!

Rabbi Lionel Blue

This recipe comes from my book Kitchen Blues *and is a favourite main course soup of mine.*

Main Course Garlic Soup
(Anglo-Welsh-Spanish version)
(serves 8)

Catherine MacIver

8 cloves garlic
4 medium potatoes
1 large onion
2 pints light stock
2 tablespoons olive oil
1 teaspoon mixed herbs
salt and freshly ground pepper

Using a saucepan, fry 4 sliced cloves of garlic in olive oil till brown. Cut up the potatoes and onion, and add, together with the remaining garlic (crushed), the stock, mixed herbs and salt and pepper to taste.

Boil, and when all the vegetables are soft, mash with a potato masher. The mixture will be rough, like the rugger players I ate it with. They came from Wales and we sang rugger songs together.

Dickie Bird

Take an Oval Bowl!

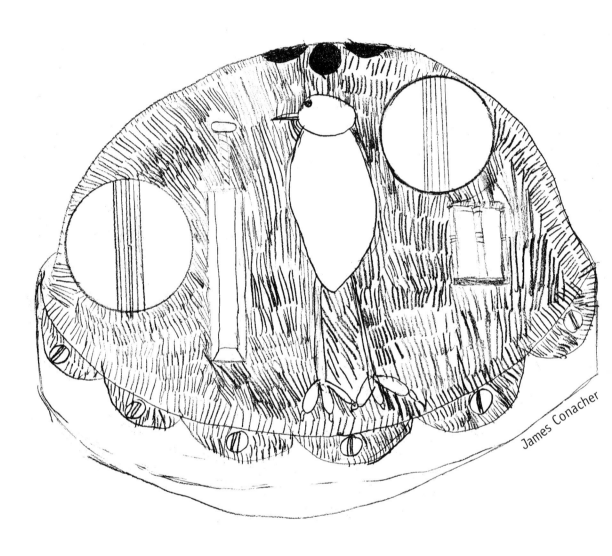

James Conacher

The silly point of this recipe is to take an oval bowl.
Assemble together 11 ingredients.
Put 2 in to beat, then add the others one at a time.
When completed, spread all 11 around the Oval and do your best
to devour the opposition!

Richie Benaud

Outback Pie

(serves 4)

1 Australian onion, finely chopped	1/2 pint rich gravy
1 lb cooked ground rump steak, or lamb	3 tsp Worcestershire sauce
2 handfuls parsley, finely chopped	1/2 tsp dried mixed herbs
salt and freshly ground black pepper	2 cups of peas, cooked
1 cup of sliced, cooked carrots	1 tsp butter
2 lbs potatoes, cooked then mashed firm	grated, mild cheese
vegetable stock (approximately	
1/2 cup if required)	

Sauté the onion in butter until tender and transparent.
Add cooked ground beef (or lamb), gravy, Worcestershire sauce, mixed herbs, salt and pepper, then the vegetable stock, if more liquid is required.
The mixture should be of a firm consistency and not runny.

On top of this place peas and carrots, cover with chopped parsley.
Cover completely with firm mashed potato.
Spread grated cheese on top.

Cook for 40–45 minutes in a medium oven until golden brown.

M.M. Kaye

Pineapple and Cream Cheese Pie

Blend 4 oz sugar with 1 tablespoon cornflour and add a 9 oz can of crushed pineapple, juice and all. Cook, stirring constantly, until the mixture is thick and clear. Cool.

Blend 8 oz of cream cheese with 4 oz sugar and 1 tsp salt. Add 2 eggs, one at a time. Stir well after each egg is added. Blend in 1/4 pt milk and 1 tsp vanilla.

Spread cooled pineapple mixture over bottom of 9 inch pastry shell. Pour in cream cheese mixture and sprinkle with 1/4 cup chopped pecans (or walnuts).

Bake in a moderately hot oven (400°F, Gas 6) for 10 minutes, then reduce heat to a very moderate oven (325°F, Gas 3) for 50 minutes. Cool before serving.

Dame Kiri Te Kanawa

Maori Kisses

(yield: 48)

4 oz butter	2 teaspoons baking powder
4 oz castor sugar	2 dessertspoons cocoa
2 eggs	1 cup chopped dates
8 oz plain flour	1 cup chopped walnuts

Time: 10–15 minutes *Temperature:* 350–375°F

Cream butter and sugar in a mixing bowl. Add eggs and beat well. Stir in sifted dry ingredients. Mix in dates and walnuts. Drop in teaspoonfuls on to cold greased baking trays. Bake in a moderate oven for 10–15 minutes. When cool, join together with Vienna icing or plain icing made by mixing sieved icing sugar with water to a smooth spreading consistency.

Vienna icing:

8 oz pure icing sugar	1 tbsp sherry
4 oz butter	4–5 drops vanilla essence

Sift icing sugar. Cream butter and add half icing sugar gradually, beating until creamy and fluffy. Beat in sherry alternately with remainder of sugar. Stir in vanilla.

© *The Australian and New Zealand Complete Book of Cookery*

Claire Fairweather

Christine Ogilvie

Tony Benn

The Cup that Cheers

Take one pint of pure water and boil it in a kettle with North Sea Gas.

Add one tea bag from the Commonwealth, some milk and sugar from the Third World and stir until the tea assumes a satisfying deep brown colour.

Then remove the tea bag and take every hour,
or more often if necessary.

Scott Cummings

Kirsty McLean

Derek Johns
33, St. James's
London W1

Roast Scallops with Braised Chicory and Maldon Salt

(1 portion)

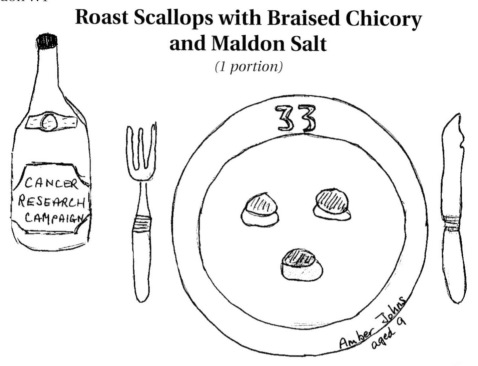

3 large scallops	2 oz butter and 1 oz clarified butter
1 head of chicory	pinch of Maldon salt
1 tbs lemon juice	3 tbs water
pepper	chervil

Remove scallops from the shells, remove roes and skirt.
Rinse very quickly under cold water and place on towel to dry.

Take the chicory, cut in half lengthways, remove middle stem and shred very finely. Place into pan with half of the water, half of the butter and half of the lemon juice. Simmer gently until tender, season and drain. Boil the rest of the water, lemon and butter and pour over the chicory.

In a very hot pan, add the clarified butter and the scallops seasoned only with pepper, sear the one side, turn over and place in a hot oven for 1 minute. The scallops should be crisp and golden on the outside and still raw in the middle.

Serve in a soup bowl with the chicory. In the middle, drizzle with a little of the lemon butter around and top with the salt crystals and chervil.

(Clarified butter is butter clear of impurities: heat butter, allowing sediment and impurities to go to the bottom of the pan, then skim off the pure oil.)

Sir Peter de la Billière

This is my standard, extensively used and tested, high calorie curry which I used to cook in mess tins throughout the jungles of the far east many years ago.

Compo Curry

Napoleon was right. An Army marches on its stomach. And this superb curry has sustained me in some very strange places around the world. Tastes best in the open air.

Heat a spoonful of ghee (it can be bought in tins, otherwise substitute vegetable oil or clarified butter) in a mess tin over a campfire, Tommy Cooker or Camping Gaz. Throw in a chopped onion and a deseeded red chilli pepper (if you're strong enough!). Fry for a few minutes, then add curry powder. Stir. Add water as necessary and garlic to taste. Stir in the meat element of an Army field ration – or an ordinary tin of meat – and anything else you happen to have around. Cook slowly to develop the flavour.

Put two man's handfuls of rice per person in another mess tin. Add twice as much water, and boil until all the water is absorbed and the rice is cooked.

Rebecca Hyland

Robin Ellis
(The Original Poldark)

Here's a soup after my own heart. I just made it this morning, which is a beautiful London morning after a light snow, blue sky and inviting. I shall eat the soup for lunch and go for a walk on Primrose Hill well fortified.

The soup comes from a totally different environment. It is a recipe from Elizabeth Romer's fascinating study of a year in the cooking life of a Tuscan farmer's wife, A Tuscan Year. It is appropriately written under the month of February (one needs constant cheering up in poor old February!) though any time in autumn or winter would be good. It is a fabulous and tasty Minestrone de Verdura – 'minestrone' means soup and 'verdura' means vegetables, so there you have it.

If you add a little drizzle of extra virgin olive oil to your soup bowl just before eating, and shut your eyes, you could enjoy it looking out from your kitchen window over the hills to the hazy outline of Florence, the city of flowers, in the far distance.

Minestrone de Verdura

1 large onion	2 large carrots, peeled
2 ribs celery with leaves	1 clove garlic, crushed (optional)
1/2 cup (120 ml) good olive oil	10 oz (300 g) white cannellini beans
9 oz (250 g) canned tomatoes	4 outer leaves green cabbage
2 large peeled potatoes	stock
parsley	salt and pepper

Chop onion, carrots and celery into small dice
(a food processor does the job quickly and efficiently).
Heat the oil in a large saucepan.
Cook these vegetables and the garlic gently until they have softened.
Add beans and mix well.
Add tomatoes, breaking them up gently as you stir them in.
Add ladle of stock (vegetable stock in cube form is fine).
Next add diced potatoes – the dice can be as small or large as you like.
Add the torn-up cabbage leaves.
Lastly add a few parsley sprigs, and a couple more ladles of stock
and season with salt and pepper.
Cook gently until all vegetables are tender – 20 minutes?

This is a thick soup where the vegetables reign suprème, but again it is up to you how much liquid you use.

© *A Tuscan Year* by Elizabeth Romer

Sally Gunnell

This is my very favourite recipe to celebrate special occasions.

Cold Chicken Curry

(serves 4)

Dylan Macdonald

4 chicken breasts, cooked and cut into bite-size pieces

Curry sauce:

1 medium onion	1 small apple, any sort
curry powder to taste	1 tbsp tomato purée
2 tbsp apricot jam	1 glass red wine
water	1 medium jar mayonnaise
vegetable oil	4 tbsp whipping cream

To decorate:

black grapes, halved   toasted flaked almonds

Chop the onion and apple, then cook gently in a little oil in a saucepan for about 5 minutes. Add curry powder, tomato purée, jam and wine. Cook until onion is soft, making sure there is enough liquid by adding water. Adjust seasoning to taste, then sieve.

Mix together the mayonnaise and cream. Add curry sauce to taste.

Pour over the chicken and place in serving dish.

Decorate with grapes around the edge and almonds scattered on top.

Serve with cold cooked rice with cucumber, spring onions, green pepper and celery cut into bite-size pieces mixed in, and crusty bread.

Lord Laing of Dunphail

Boeuf Bourguignon
(serves 4–6)

2 lb stewing steak, cut into 2 1/2 inch squares
3 tablespoons lard, or alternative cooking fat
3 1/2 oz salt pork, cut into squares
12 small onions
1 tablespoon flour
2 cups Burgundy (as good a quality as you can bear to use!)
1 clove garlic, a bouquet tied together of about 2 inches of orange peel, a bay leaf, a small sprig of thyme, a sliver of nutmeg. Salt, no pepper.

Melt the fat in a flameproof casserole, until very hot. Brown salt pork and remove. Brown onions and remove. Brown meat on all sides. Add salt pork and flour, stirring with a wooden spoon. Add the wine, well heated, stir well. Add garlic and bouquet. Cover hermetically and cook over low flame for 3 1/2 hours. Add more water if necessary, but only a small quantity. Add onions and cook for a further 15 minutes. Remove bouquet, season to taste with salt, and serve.

Prue Leith

Caledonian-Chinese Beef Stir-Fry
(serves 2)

8 oz / 225 g rump steak, cut into thin strips
2 tablespoons oil
1 tablespoon Scotch whisky
1 large clove of garlic, crushed
1 inch fresh ginger, peeled and chopped
1 x 8 oz / 225 g tin water chestnuts, drained and sliced
4 spring onions, chopped

For the marinade:
4 tablespoons light soy sauce
2 teaspoons sesame oil
1 tablespoon runny honey

Mix the marinade ingredients together, add the beef and refrigerate overnight.
Drain the meat, reserving the marinade.
Heat the oil in a wok or frying pan. Stir-fry the beef fast to brown.
Add the whisky. Turn up heat to evaporate liquid. Set alight if you like!
Add the garlic, ginger and chestnuts and stir-fry fast.
Tip into a dish and sprinkle on the spring onions.

Sir George Christie
Glyndebourne

Tesco Pork Sausages for Me and the Pugs

6 Tesco pork and mustard sausages cooked in a Pyrex dish with a dribble of water covering the base of the dish for 20 minutes in a very hot oven, served with thin American frizzled bacon – and shared with the pugs as a tele-snack with a good Prom concert for me or a wildlife programme for the pugs.

Willie Carson

Penne with Smoked Salmon

(serves 4–6)

12 oz smoked salmon offcuts   1 lb penne (pasta)   9 tbsp vodka

1/2 pt double cream   salt and black pepper

Cut salmon into small pieces.
Cook pasta al dente.
Drain. Place back into pan.
At the last moment heat vodka and cream until almost boiling, add salmon.
Mix all ingredients with pasta and season well.
Serve and enjoy.

Jane Churchill

Chocolate Sauce

2 oz butter
2 tablespoons icing sugar
2 tablespoons cocoa
2 tablespoons golden syrup

Put all ingredients into a saucepan and stir until hot.

Anton Edelmann
Maître Chef des Cuisines, The Savoy Hotel

Lemon Crêpe Gâteau

The idea of cold pancakes may be alarming but they make a surprisingly good base for this unusual gâteau.

7 eggs
300g (10 oz) caster sugar
180ml (6 fl oz) lemon juice
60g (2 oz) unsalted butter, diced
30g (1 oz) powdered or leaf gelatine
100ml (3 1/2 fl oz) water
400ml (14 fl oz) double cream, lightly whipped
icing sugar for dusting

For the crêpes:
100g (3 1/2 fl oz) plain flour
pinch of salt
2 eggs
4 tbsp caster sugar
300ml (1/2 pint) milk
45g (1 1/2 oz) butter

For the crêpes, sift the flour and salt into a large bowl, then add the eggs, sugar and about a quarter of the milk and mix to a thick batter. Slowly add the rest of the milk to give a thin pouring batter. If there are any lumps in it, pass it through a fine sieve. Melt the butter in a pan until it begins to foam and then whisk half of it into the batter. Leave to rest in a cool place for 15 minutes.

Heat a 20cm (8 inch) non-stick omelette pan, brush with a little of the remaining melted butter, then ladle in enough batter to cover the base of the pan in a thin layer, tilting the pan gently so the batter spreads evenly. Cook for 30 seconds over a medium-high heat until browned, then turn over and cook for a further 30 seconds. Continue making pancakes in this way until all the batter is used up. There should be 10 pancakes.

Place the eggs, sugar and lemon juice in a heavy-based pan and bring just to the boil over a gentle heat, whisking constantly. Remove from the heat and stir in the butter until it has melted.

Put the gelatine and water in a pan, soak for 10 minutes, then heat gently to dissolve. Add a little of the lemon mousse, mix well, then fold in the remaining mousse. Leave to cool. Fold in the lightly whipped cream.

Lightly grease the base and sides of a 23cm (9 inch) round spring-release tin, and line with cling film. Use 4–5 pancakes to line the base and sides of the tin, reserving 2 for the top, then layer the lemon mousse and remaining pancakes. Finish with one reserved pancake, fold in overlapping edges, and top with the other pancake. Cover and chill for at least 4 hours, preferably overnight, until set. Unmould and dust with icing sugar.

Tricia Guild
Designers Guild

Louise Chappell

Spaghetti with Raw Tomato and Rocket

(serves 2)

Cook the spaghetti in plenty of salted boiling water. Meanwhile sauté 1 chopped clove of garlic in oil, then add 8 roughly chopped plum tomatoes. Allow to heat through without cooking and add 1 tablespoon of toasted chopped almonds and a large handful of chopped fresh rocket leaves. Toss with the drained spaghetti and serve at once. Season with salt and pepper to taste.

Louise Chappell

Nick Faldo

A Hole In One

Being British through and through, I have to say that my most favourite meal is roast lamb – especially when it has been cooked by my Mum!

And another of my favourite easy-to-prepare meals is called 'A Hole In One'. What is it? Basically, it is a bowl of creamed mashed potatoes with a hole scooped from the middle which I then fill in one fell swoop with bangers and beans. There you have it!

Vikki Robb

Lucinda Green

Lucinda's Chicken

(serves 4)

1 cooked chicken, cut into pieces.
Combine 1 pint of whipping cream,
mushroom ketchup, Worcestershire
sauce and mango chutney to taste.
Pour over chicken pieces in flat oven-
proof dish and heat until warmed
through in medium oven. Don't let cream sauce boil.

The Rt. Hon. William Hague, M.P.

Steamed Treacle Sponge with Custard

Ingredients:

2–3 tbsp golden syrup	2 eggs
4 oz butter or hard margarine	4 oz caster sugar
4 oz self raising flour	2 tbsp cold water or milk
1 tsp ground ginger (optional)	
grated rind of 1 lemon (optional)	

Method:
Butter a 1 1/2 pt pudding basin.
Pour golden syrup into the bottom of the basin.
Cream the butter and sugar together until light and fluffy.
Beat in the eggs and cold water or milk (and lemon rind if used).
Carefully fold in the flour (sifted with the ginger if used).
Spoon into the basin and cover with a circle of buttered foil pleated in the middle
so that there is enough room to allow the pudding to rise.
Seal well around the brim of the basin so that no steam can get into the pudding.
Place in a steamer over boiling water and steam for about 1 1/2 hours.
Check level of water in the bottom of the steamer from time to time.
When cooked turn on to a warm dish and serve with custard.

The Rt. Hon. Sebastian Coe, M.P.

Traditional Cornish Pasty

Heat oven to 400°F / 200°C

Ingredients:
10 oz shortcrust pastry
8 oz chuck steak
1 medium onion
pepper and salt
knob of butter
8 oz potatoes and swede
   (called turnip in Cornwall)
beaten egg or milk (optional)

Method:
Chop meat, onion, potatoes and swede into very small pieces. Roll out pastry, cut out four rounds. Place filling on one half of each circle in this order – mixed potatoes and swede, meat, then onion, season. Place knob of butter on top. Moisten edges of pastry and fold over to cover mixture. Press edges together firmly and crimp edges. Place on a baking tray.   Make a ventilating hole. Brush with beaten egg or milk if glaze is required. Cook in hot oven for about 30 minutes or until pale brown. Turn down heat to 350°F / 180°C for a further 25–30 minutes. (Cover with foil if becoming too brown.)

P.S. A little moisture (stock) can be added but very carefully or juices will run out (in Cornwall "come abroad"). Vegetables can be used in vegetarian dishes, i.e. onion, leeks, swede, grated carrot, potatoes.

Antonio Carluccio
The Neal Street Restaurant
26 Neal Street
London WC2H 9PS
Tel: 0171 836 8368

Nocciole d'Agnello con Carciofi
(Noisette of Lamb with Artichokes)
(serves 4)

Noisettes are the most tender cut of lamb and, in this recipe, they should be accompanied by equally tender artichokes. It is during the spring that you will be able to find these tender artichokes, which in Pinzimonio can even be eaten raw. If you are unable to obtain any of these, you may substitute artichoke hearts.

4 small artichokes
400g (14 oz) lamb fillet (sirloin or noisette)
1 tbs capers, preferably salted
1 bunch of spring onions (scallions)
4 tbs olive oil
50g (2 oz) prosciutto crudo, with fat, cut into strips
a ladle of stock
2 tbs chopped parsley
salt and freshly ground black pepper
a slice of lemon

Wash the artichokes and pull off the tough outside leaves. Trim off the tops and cut into quarters. If the artichokes have spiny centres, remove these with a sharp knife. Put aside in a bowl of cold water with a slice of lemon.

Cut the lamb fillet into 2 cm (1 inch) thick noisettes. Put the capers to soak in cold water to wash off surplus salt or vinegar. Chop the spring onions. Now heat the olive oil in a medium-sized saucepan and fry the noisettes, turning them over so that they brown on each side, remove them from the pan and place them in a hot dish to keep warm.

Add to the pan the spring onions and the prosciutto cut into strips, fry briefly over a strong flame and then add the pieces of artichoke. Stir-fry all together for 5 or 6 minutes. Now add a ladle of stock and the capers, turn the heat down and cook gently for a further 10–15 minutes or until the artichokes are cooked.

Return the noisettes to the pan, add the parsley, black pepper and salt (if necessary), mix the meat together with the artichokes and serve straight away.

Carluccio's Food Shop is to be found at 28A Neal Street, tel: 0171 240 1487.
© Antonio Carluccio, *An Invitation to Italian Cooking*, Pavilion, 1986

Sir Terence Conran

Steak and Kidney Pudding

(Serves 6)

1 1/2 lb (700g) beef – two-thirds chuck, one-third skirt
1/2 lb (225g) ox kidney
1–2 tbsp flour, seasoned with salt and pepper
2 shallots
1/4 lb (115g) button mushrooms, washed and trimmed
1 tsp each of anchovy essence, Worcester sauce,
    mushroom ketchup and tomato purée
small glass of red wine
salt and freshly ground pepper

For the suet crust:
1/2 lb (225g) self-raising flour
1/4 lb (115g) shredded suet
salt and freshly ground pepper

Method:
Cut the beef into pieces about 1/2 in/1 cm across, trimming away fat and sinews. Remove the central core from the kidney and cut it into pieces about the same size. Roll the meat thoroughly in the seasoned flour. Peel and chop the shallots. Mix meat, mushrooms and shallots in a bowl.

Next make the suet crust. Mix the flour, suet, salt and pepper in a bowl and add 7–8 tablespoons cold water to make a pliable dough. Roll out two-thirds of the dough on a floured board, and use it to line a greased pudding basin.

Pile the beef, mushrooms, kidney and chopped shallots into the lined bowl. Mix the anchovy essence, Worcestershire sauce, mushroom ketchup, tomato purée, wine, salt and pepper, and 1/2 pt water in a jug. Pour it into the pudding, adding enough extra cold water to come just below the top of the meat. Roll out the remaining pastry into a round. Brush one side of it with water, and put it loosely over the top of the meat, damp side down, pressing well around the edges with your fingers to seal it to the lower half of the pastry. Trim away any excess pastry from the edges. Take a large round of greaseproof paper, grease it on one side, and place it loosely over the pudding. Put an even larger round of foil loosely over this, and tie tightly with string just below the rim of the pudding basin. Tie a string handle across the top of the basin so that it can be removed easily at the end. Take a large saucepan with a well-fitting lid, and half fill it with water (to which you can add a dash of vinegar to prevent staining the saucepan with long boiling).

Bring the water to the boil and lower in the pudding – the water should come about 1 in/2.5 cm below the string. Cover the pan – this is most important – and boil gently for 4 hours 30 minutes, topping up with more boiling water as necessary.

To serve the pudding, lift it out of the pan, remove the foil and greaseproof paper and pin a neatly folded white napkin around the bowl. Put it on a plate, place it on the table, and plunge in the serving spoon to release a cloud of scented steam.

Nick Faldo's
"A Hole in One"
(p.49)

Ruth Johnston

Jackie Stewart's
"Roast Chicken with Almonds & Honey"
(p.89)

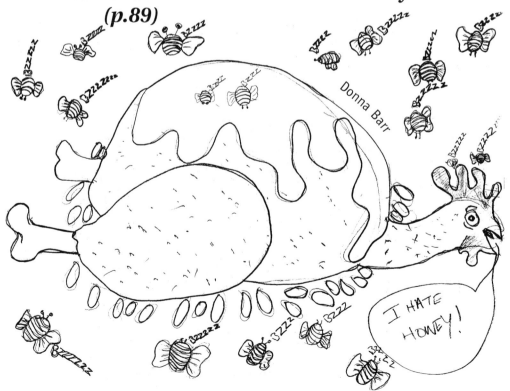

Donna Barr

The Most Rev. the Rt. Hon. Dr. George Carey, Archbishop of Canterbury

Chicken Toscana

(serves 4)

3 lb roasting chicken	1 onion
1 carrot	bouquet garni
3/4 pt water	salt and pepper
4 oz mushrooms	1 small cucumber
1 dsrtsp arrowroot	1 tbsp snipped chives

Simmer the chicken gently in the water with the vegetables, herbs and seasoning until tender – about 45–50 minutes.

In the meantime, chop the mushrooms finely, peel the cucumber and cut into quarters lengthwise and then cut into 2 inch pieces. Blanch the cucumber and drain well.

Strain the stock from the chicken when cooked and add to another saucepan. Boil the stock to reduce by about half its original quantity.

Add mushrooms and simmer for about 3 minutes.

Take the chicken and carve into neat joints and arrange in a serving dish.

Mix the arrowroot with a little stock and add to the pan. Stir until boiling. Add the chives and cucumber. Spoon over the chicken and serve at once.

Serve with boiled new potatoes and green vegetables.

Michael Barry
The Crafty Cook

Gratin of Winter Vegetables
(serves 4)

This can be eaten as a vegetarian dish on its own, or with sausages or grilled meats, with which it is particularly good as it has a nice rich sauce. A "gratin", by the way, gets its name from the delicious crusty burnt bits which stick to the lid of the cooking dish and used to be scraped off and eaten (from the French "gratter", to scrape).

Ingredients:
1/2 pt (300 ml) milk (not skimmed)
1 1/2 oz (40 g) cornflour
1 oz (25 g) butter
alpine salt and freshly ground black pepper
grated nutmeg – optional
1/2 lb (225 g) each leeks, carrots and parsnips
4 oz (110 g) grated cheese – Gruyère or Cheddar
4 oz (110 g) fresh breadcrumbs

Method:
Make the white sauce first. Use a non-stick saucepan and a good whisk. Put in the milk, butter and flour, and whisk together. Heat until it goes thick, whisking every now again – do not walk away and answer the phone – then add a good pinch of salt (and nutmeg, if you are using it), and pepper. Whisk again and put to one side.

You now have a thick, creamy, shiny white sauce.

Prepare the vegetables. Peel the carrots and parsnips, wash the leeks carefully and cut them into 1-inch (2.5 cm) chunks. Bring a big saucepan of salted water to the boil. Put all the vegetables in together and boil them for just 5 minutes. You are not softening them, just blanching them. Drain the vegetables and put them into a gratin or baking dish – anything that is round, square or oval with a flat bottom and about an inch and a half (4 cm) deep. Pour the white sauce over them and sprinkle on the grated cheese and breadcrumbs. Put it either under a grill (but not too close to the heat) for about 10 minutes, or into a hot oven, gas mark 6/400°F/200°C/180° fan-assisted oven, or the top of an Aga roasting oven for approximately 20 minutes until the top is bubbling and golden.

This dish is succulent and gorgeous – the leeks are green, the parsnips give sweetness and the carrots give crunch. I actually like it as a main course, served with wholemeal bread and butter, but you can serve it as a splendid side dish.

Michael Barry
The Crafty Cook

Chinese Chicken and Peppers
(serves 4)

This is a dish to stir-fry. It is usually made in a wok, but a large frying pan is fine, preferably non-stick. It is very, very easy to make. The secret is to get the pan very hot before you put anything in it.

Ingredients:
1 lb (450 g) boneless chicken meat –
    thighs are fine for this, breasts if you want to splash out!
1 red pepper, 1 green pepper and 1 Spanish onion

For the sauce:
2 tbsp each of soy sauce and water
1 tsp each of brown sugar, cornflour and lemon juice

Method:
The great trick with Chinese food is to cut everything to the same size, and to have a good, broad spatula to make the stir-frying even easier. Wash the red and green peppers, and take out the seeds and white bits inside. Peel the onion and slice into half-inch (1 cm) slices, and do the same with the peppers. Cut the chicken meat against the grain into the same sort of sized pieces. Heat the oil in the pan until it is almost smoking. Put in the chicken and fry it quickly. The pieces are quite small so it should take about 4–5 minutes. Push it to the side of the pan and add the onions and the peppers. Stir those and fry for another 3 or 4 minutes. The chicken, meanwhile, is quietly cooking on the side of the pan. In a cup, stir together the soy sauce, water, brown sugar, cornflour and lemon juice. Mix until it is a really smooth mixture, then pour into the pan and toss the whole lot together. It looks a bit unpromising for the first 10 seconds, then suddenly the cornflour starts to work and the sauce goes thick and glossy and coats everything. All those wonderful colours, tastes and textures are covered in the marvellous sweet and sour sauce. Serve it immediately the sauce has thickened and gone glossy, with lots of plain boiled rice.

Michael Caine

Carrot Cake

2 cups plain flour	2 cups sugar	4 eggs
2 oz butter	2 cups grated carrots	1 cup raisins
1 cup walnuts	1 tsp cinnamon	1 tsp ginger
nutmeg	vanilla essence	2 tsp baking powder

Method:
Mix butter and sugar until creamy. Add one egg with a little flour. Then add carrots to mixing bowl and all other ingredients. Bake for 40 minutes at 350°F.

Joan Collins

Pasta Primavera

(serves 4 people)

Once spurned by dieters, there has been a rethink on pasta and it is now recognised as an excellent source of complex carbohydrates and one of the perfect energy foods. Choose whole wheat pasta as it contains fibre, and serve it with a light tomato and herb sauce, but do not be tempted into topping it with a rich, or cream, sauce high in calories.

Here is one of my favourite recipes for pasta:

500g penne	8 large mushrooms
1 broccoli head	2 large tomatoes
2 medium-sized courgettes	2 cloves of garlic
2 medium-sized onions	grated parmesan cheese (optional)
salt and pepper	

Cook the pasta in boiling water for 12 minutes (until al dente). Drain and refresh with boiling water (removing excess starch). Break the broccoli head into florets and cook in a steamer or colander over boiling water. Steam for 7 minutes approximately (so that the broccoli is cooked, but still crunchy).

Chop the onions coarsely and sauté in a little butter until soft. (If you have a microwave no butter is needed. Put the onions in a bowl with about half an inch of water on the bottom. Cover with cling film and cook at a high temperature for two and a half minutes. When cooked, drain and add to the broccoli.)

Wash the courgettes and cut into 2" strips. Cook in the steamer for about 5 minutes or boil in water until cooked but not too soft.

Clean the mushrooms with a little salt and kitchen paper (or you can peel them). Place under a hot grill for a few minutes. Drain on kitchen paper. When cooked, cut into large chunks.

Concasse the tomatoes by placing them in boiling water for 10 seconds, then transferring them immediately to cold water. This allows you to remove the skin. Quarter, and cut each quarter in half again. Remove the seeds.

Crush the garlic and add to the vegetables. Season with salt and pepper. Add the vegetables (except the broccoli) to the pasta and reheat gently in a saucepan.

Place the broccoli back in the steamer for a minute to reheat and then carefully add to the hot pasta and vegetables. This prevents the broccoli from breaking up.

Add a little grated parmesan for more flavour but this is not essential. Serve warm – not too hot. It's scrumptious and another healthy dish that children will savour.

Ted Hughes
Poet Laureate

I have a liking for wild venison, but I can never find it as I really want it – except in my own home.

Wild Venison

Now and again, I buy a big piece – half an animal – sika, fallow, roe or red hind, in that order of preference. In this recipe red stag is pretty good and bought in bulk it's reasonably cheap. I butcher the whole piece, or bone it out, and pack the different cuts into different bags for freezing. When the time comes for a feast, I always open a variety of bags and mix up the different cuts.

My marinade consists of a reasonable quality port topped up with what I consider very good Rioja. I also use game stock if there's any around. With large quantities of meat, seasoning becomes more creative. I throw in a great deal of garlic, bay leaves, herbs as they seem right, peppercorns, spices, pepper and sliced onions. A lot of this is somewhere between improvisation and blind faith. I leave salt to the diners.

I marinade the meat for 24 hours at least, perhaps turning it once or twice. Then I dry the meat on kitchen roll before dropping it into my hot butter and maybe some olive oil, to fry the surfaces and seal it. Once it's browned, I take it out and add flour to the butter and mix to make a gravy. Back in with the meat and the marinade. Maybe two big pans of it going now and at this point I add a few other things, never forgetting the main thing – pickled walnuts. Maybe more onions, lemon juice, last minute spice.

Once this lot comes to the boil, I pour it into big pyrex bowls, or earthenware jars, and push it into the oven at a low heat for several hours. It emerges as a black mass of steaming and breaking collops, and is eaten with mashed potato and redcurrant or other tasty jelly.

It sounds like a crude sort of dish and I suppose it is. However, it does have one great quality which is that in my experience many human beings go crazy for it!

Lara Bernays

Neil Haidar
Masterchef 1996

Fennel Risotto

(serves 4)

Bulb fennel, also known as Florence fennel, is now widely available in British supermarkets. Although it can be eaten raw, it becomes truly delicious when browned in olive oil and cooked until tender. Combine it with risotto rice and freshly grated Parmesan and you have a wonderful dish for the cold winter months.

3 tbsp extra virgin olive oil
300g fennel, diced
1 clove garlic, finely chopped
300g risotto rice (arborio or,
   preferably, carnaroli)
1.5 litres good chicken stock (or use
   3 chicken stock cubes) at boiling point

2 tbsp pastis (Pernod)
50g unsalted butter
50g freshly grated Parmesan
salt and pepper

Method:
Heat the oil in a wide, heavy-based saucepan over a high heat. Lightly brown the diced fennel, then reduce the heat to medium and sauté the garlic for 30 seconds. Add the rice and stir, ensuring that all the grains are coated with oil. Fry for a further minute before adding the stock, a ladleful at a time. As each ladleful of stock is absorbed, keep adding more until the rice is almost cooked (about 20 minutes). Add the pastis, and a little more stock if necessary, and cook until al dente, i.e. still slightly firm to the bite but with no trace of chalkiness at the centre of the grains. Season with salt and pepper. Remove the pan from the heat, stir in the butter and Parmesan and allow to rest, covered, for 3 minutes. Serve in warmed soup bowls, with extra grated Parmesan.

Susan Hampshire

Susan's Salad

(serves 2)

On a bed of lettuce or chicory:
1 banana, chopped
2 carrots, grated
2 tomatoes, sliced
handful of raisins
cottage cheese or mild goat's cheese
pineapple or strawberries
6 almonds
grated ginger root (optional)

Dressing:
chopped chives and parsley
walnut oil
1 tsp lemon juice or cider vinegar
onion salt to taste
ground pepper

Arrange all the ingredients on the bed of lettuce or chicory. Grate the ginger root (if used) onto the cheese. Mix the ingredients for the dressing and pour over.

The Rt. Hon. Michael Heseltine, M.P.

Fillets of Turbot and Salmon
Wrapped in Japanese Seaweed and Steamed
Served with a sweet and sour beetroot sauce
(serves 2)

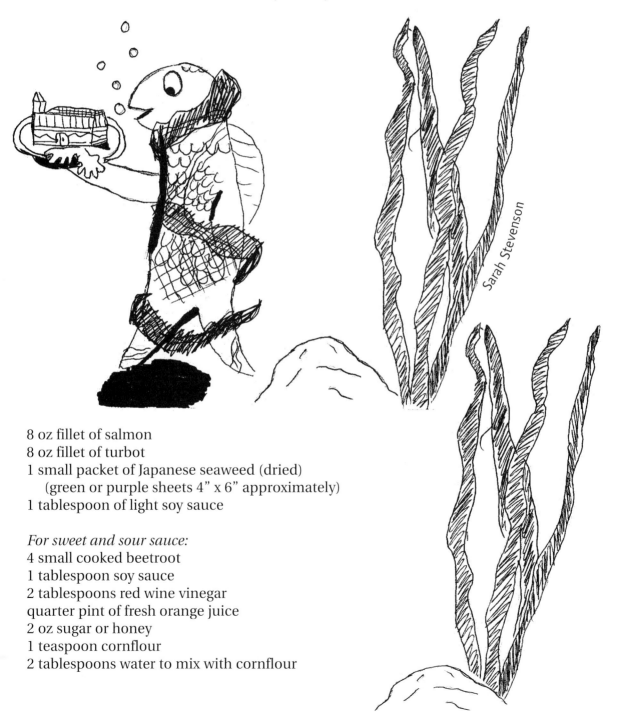

8 oz fillet of salmon
8 oz fillet of turbot
1 small packet of Japanese seaweed (dried)
    (green or purple sheets 4" x 6" approximately)
1 tablespoon of light soy sauce

For sweet and sour sauce:
4 small cooked beetroot
1 tablespoon soy sauce
2 tablespoons red wine vinegar
quarter pint of fresh orange juice
2 oz sugar or honey
1 teaspoon cornflour
2 tablespoons water to mix with cornflour

The Rt. Hon. Michael Heseltine, M.P.'s *Fillets of Turbot and Salmon continued*

Method:
Trim fish to approximately 4 inches long by 1 inch wide.
Marinade in soy sauce for a couple of hours.

Spray seaweed with water to soften.

Place strips of fish on top of one sheet of softened seaweed and roll up into a cigar shape. Next wrap each in clingfilm and steam for approximately 15 minutes.

Grate beetroot and place in saucepan with all other ingredients for sauce (apart from cornflour and water). Bring to the boil and then simmer for 20 minutes.
Strain the mixture and then thicken with the cornflour and water.

When fish is cooled, remove from the clingfilm and slice each into 5 pieces.

This can be served on a bed of stir-fried beansprouts with garlic and ginger surrounded by the beetroot sauce.

Tim Henman

Banana Cheesecake

2 oz butter/margarine   5 oz plain chocolate-coated digestive biscuits

Crush the biscuits. Melt the butter and stir in the crumbs. Press over the bottom of a greased loose-bottomed 7–8 inch tin. Chill.

2 ripe bananas	juice of 1/2 lemon	1 tbsp sugar
8 oz cream cheese	1/4 pt soured cream	1 egg
1/2 oz powdered gelatine		5 tbsp water

In a blender, mix the cream cheese and soured cream until smooth. Add the sugar, lemon juice and egg and blend again. Break up the bananas, add and blend until smooth. Dissolve the gelatine in the water and mix in. Chill for 3–4 hours until the filling is set.

Curd cheese may be substituted for the cream cheese; similarly yogurt can be used instead of the soured cream.

Lenny Henry

Lenny Henry's Killer Chilli

Ingredients:

1 lb minced beef
2 big onions
2 green peppers
1 tin Italian tomatoes
1 tin kidney beans
tomato purée
chilli powder – mild or not,
    depending on whether your
    tongue is made of leather!
pinch of oregano
pinch of mixed spices
pinch of cloves
dash of Tabasco
glass of red wine
2 beef Oxo cubes
1/4 lb mushrooms
butter for frying
lucky rabbit's foot!

Cooking instructions:

Place rabbit's foot round your neck (you're going to need all the luck you can get because I certainly don't know what I'm doing!).

Chop onions and green peppers. Fry in about 4 oz butter until they are fairly translucent (that means see-through, thicky). Add the meat and fry until it is brown. Add the tomatoes and stir for a couple of minutes until it is bubbling noisily. Add tomato purée (about 1 tbsp) and stir until sauce thickens. Add all the spices and herbs, chop mushrooms, add them and stir for 2 minutes. Add kidney beans and give it a good stir. Add dash of Tabasco and crumble in Oxo cubes and wine and stir again. Put on a low heat, e.g. Gas Mark 2, and simmer for about one hour, stirring occasionally. After this time it should be a lovely dark brown colour and quite thick. If there is a layer of fat on top, scrape off with a spoon.

Yum Yum in my Tum!

Serve with rice or pitta bread to about 4 people.

Stephen Hendry

Sweet and Sour Chicken

(serves 4)

4 chicken portions
2 x 15 ml spoons dripping or oil
1 x 200 g can pineapple rings
2 x 15 ml spoons soy sauce
2 x 15 ml spoons tomato
    ketchup
1 x 15 ml spoon wine vinegar
1 x 15 ml spoon soft brown sugar
1 onion, peeled and sliced
1 x 15 ml spoon plain flour
1 x 425 g can tomatoes
salt and freshly ground black
    pepper
1 red or green pepper, cored,
    seeded and sliced
freshly boiled rice to serve

Preparation time: 10 minutes
Cooking time: about 1 hour
Oven: 180°C, 350°F, Gas Mark 4

Connie

Method:
Season chicken portions all over with salt and pepper. Heat the dripping or oil in a frying pan, add the chicken and fry until well browned all over. Transfer to a casserole.

Drain the pineapple, reserving the syrup. Chop two rings and sprinkle over the chicken. Reserve the remaining pineapple for the garnish. Make up the syrup to 150 ml/1/4 pt with water. Add the soy sauce, ketchup, vinegar and sugar to the syrup.

Add the onion and red or green pepper to the frying pan and fry in the same fat until tender. Stir in the flour and cook for 1 minute, then add the pineapple syrup mixture and tomatoes and bring to the boil, stirring well. Add salt and pepper to taste and simmer for 2 minutes. Pour over the chicken.

Cover the casserole and cook in a preheated oven for about 45 minutes or until the chicken is tender. Serve with freshly boiled rice and garnish each piece of chicken with half a pineapple ring.

Mark Hix
Executive Chef – The Ivy and Le Caprice

Salmon Fishcakes with Sorrel Sauce

(serves 4–8)

For the fishcakes:
650 g mashed potato, no cream or butter added
650 g salmon fillet, poached in fish stock and flaked
2 tbsp tomato ketchup
2 tbsp anchovy essence
3 tbsp English mustard
salt and freshly ground pepper

For the sauce:
1/2 ltr strong fish stock
50 g butter
30 g flour
50 ml white wine
250 ml double cream
15 g fresh sorrel, shredded
salt and pepper

1.5 kg spinach, picked over, washed
and dried

To make the fishcakes, mix together the potato, half the poached salmon, the ketchup, anchovy essence, mustard and seasoning until it is smooth. Fold in the rest of the salmon. Mould the mixture into 8 round cakes and refrigerate.

To make the sauce, bring the fish stock to the boil in a thick-bottomed pan. In another pan melt the butter and stir in the flour. Cook very slowly over a low heat for 30 seconds, then gradually whisk in the fish stock. Pour in the white wine and simmer gently for 30 minutes until the sauce has thickened. Add the cream and reduce the sauce until it is of a thick pouring consistency, then put in the sorrel and season.

Preheat the oven to 200°C / gas mark 6. Lightly flour the fishcakes and fry them until they are coloured on both sides, then bake them for 10–15 minutes.

Heat a large saucepan over a medium flame, add the spinach, season it lightly and cover tightly with a lid. Cook for 3–4 minutes, stirring occasionally, until the leaves are tender. Drain in a colander.

Put some spinach on each plate, then a fishcake and pour over the sauce. Serve immediately.

House of Lords

7 August 97

Dear Mrs Pinckney:

Your celebrity Cookbook.

Thank you for your letter of 4 August.

I am sorry to say that, since at the time your new cookbook comes out, I shall be 90 years of age, there is no chance of my being able to add to your collection of recipes.

But I wish it, and you, and the Cancer Research campaign every possible success.

Yrs: sincerely:

Hailsham of St Marylebone

Lady Macdonald of Macdonald
Kinloch Lodge, Isle of Skye

Stuffing for Turkey

This can be made and frozen, packed into a large polythene bag and labelled clearly – it is frightening how anonymous frozen items are! Thaw for 24 hours before stuffing the turkey, any leftover stuffing is delicious cold.

This amount is for a turkey weighing about 12–15 lb:

3 lb good pork sausages – I use M & S Lincoln sausages for this
2 onions, skinned and finely chopped
3 tablespoons sunflower oil
2 cloves of garlic, skinned and finely chopped
1 lb pinhead oatmeal

grated rind of 1 washed and dried lemon
a pinch of dried thyme
1/2 teaspoon salt, plenty of ground black pepper
3 Granny Smith apples, peeled and cored, and chopped

Heat the oil in a large frying or sauté pan, and cook the chopped onions till they are transparent looking. Then add the chopped garlic and the oatmeal, and cook, stirring slowly, for a further few minutes. Season with the grated lemon rind, the salt, pepper and thyme. Then take this mixture off the heat and cool completely.

With a sharp knife slit down each sausage – the skins peel off easily. Put the skinned sausages into a large bowl, add the chopped apples, and mix in the cooled oatmeal mixture. Pack into a large polythene bag, label and freeze.

Marion Macfarlane
Masterchef 1995

Fillet of Highland Hare with Wild Mushrooms in a Creamy Marsala Sauce
(serves 4)

2 saddles of hare
hazelnut oil
6 oz mixed mushrooms
8 morels (soaked for 30 minutes in warm water)
2 tsp oil
1 1/2 oz unsalted butter
4 fl oz Marsala
5 fl oz double cream
salt and pepper
1/2 pt of previously made hare stock and a little of the morel soaking water
leeks and chervil, to serve

Marion Macfarlane's *Fillet of Highland Hare continued*

Prior to cooking, remove the fillets and the tiny fillets mignon and marinade in hazelnut oil for about 24 hours. The carcass can be used to make the hare stock. Slice all the mushrooms and set aside. Season the fillets and heat oil and half the butter in a frying pan till hot, then sear the fillets on both sides. Depending on the size, this should take about 3–5 minutes. The fillets should still be quite pink. Remove and keep warm. Pour off the fat, add the remaining butter and sauté the mushrooms for a few minutes and season. Remove and keep warm. Add the stock and a little morel water and reduce till almost half, then add the Marsala and reduce again. When the alcohol has evaporated, add the cream and reduce till the sauce thickens. Add the morels and heat through. Carve the fillets into 6–7 collops and arrange in a circle around a mound of stir-fry leeks. Decorate with mixed mushrooms and spoon over the sauce. Place a forcemeat ball on top of the leeks and decorate with chervil.

Note: Depending on the season I sometimes use a mixture of wild (chanterelle, boletus, pied de mouton, etc.) and cultivated mushrooms. If wild mushrooms are unavailable I use chestnut mushrooms and add 1 oz dried ceps.

Forcemeat Balls

2 oz hare meat
1 dsrtsp double cream

2 oz chestnut mushrooms
salt and pepper

I use the fillet mignons and the ends trimmed from the fillets.

Process the meat and the mushrooms till finely chopped, then add the cream. Season well and roll into four balls. Keep cool till needed. Cook for 5–6 minutes at 190°C until set.

69

Maureen Lipman

How to Give the Perfect Dinner Party

First allow guest guilt to build up to the point where you spend most of your time at social functions behind the drapes, your husband or, preferably, someone else's husband. Then make a list of people to whom you owe invitations. When you've filled 2 exercise books throw them away and invite, instead, people you've just met and wish to suck up to.

Next pick an evening which suits everyone and has an empty day before it in the diary. Over the subsequent days, fill up the said day with appointments, including some which necessitate leaving town via British Rail and some which require physical exertion, i.e., agree to abseil over Coventry Cathedral in aid of Distressed Single Lady Accountants.

As the day approaches, select a menu at 3.30 in the morning under the influence of drugs and remember you are appearing on Breakfast TV in 3 hours' time on a discussion panel about "how to prevent under-eye bags". Leave instructions with the inmates of the house to buy last-minute ingredients such as several chickens stuffed with chestnuts between skin and flesh marinaded in herbed wine for 24 hours and home-made mango and coconut icecream. Leave note for daily lady to turn off the water running on the frozen smoked trout before it's pummelled into a trout purée and set table with what's left of best china.

Return in good time to bail out the kitchen and read note reminding me of half-day closing in Muswell Hill. Pausing to drink half-bottle of dry sherry, run to last remaining open supermarket, to purchase frozen fish fillets, oven chips, sliced bread, various tins and trifle with dodgy sell-by date stuck over even dodgier sell-by date and warm Sauvignon. Place wine in microwave and frozen fish in freezer, take all your clothes off and apply face pack whilst running bath. Whilst in bath remember what you've done and race down naked to reverse the contents of freezer and microwave. Body should now be mottled red from bath and nipples akimbo from freezer as your Friday gardener (own key) pops in for his £50. Only when he leaves and you try to put your purse in your pocket do you realise how you looked when you were discussing the lupins with him.

Wearing face pack and dressing gown, flour and season defrosted fish and place on table and put chips in oven-proof dish. Heat oil and oven. Tip M. and S. tomato and herb soup from tins to saucepan and add own herbs to point of lunacy. Likewise mushy peas. Spread copies of this week's papers on serving counter and butter thickly on slices of bread. Open jars of pickled onions, beetroot, gherkins and bottle of HP sauce. Add vinegar, salt and pepper, linen napkins and best glasses. Throw on little black dress and as door bell rings, oil bursts into flame, bottle in freezer explodes and cat eats trifle, smile brightly, cracking face pack into 4,000 wrinkles and open door to first guest.

Ally McCoist

Succulent Soccer Stew or Humble Pie
(My favourite stew)

Serves 11 (plus two substitutes if required)

Seated in 4. 2. 4 formation

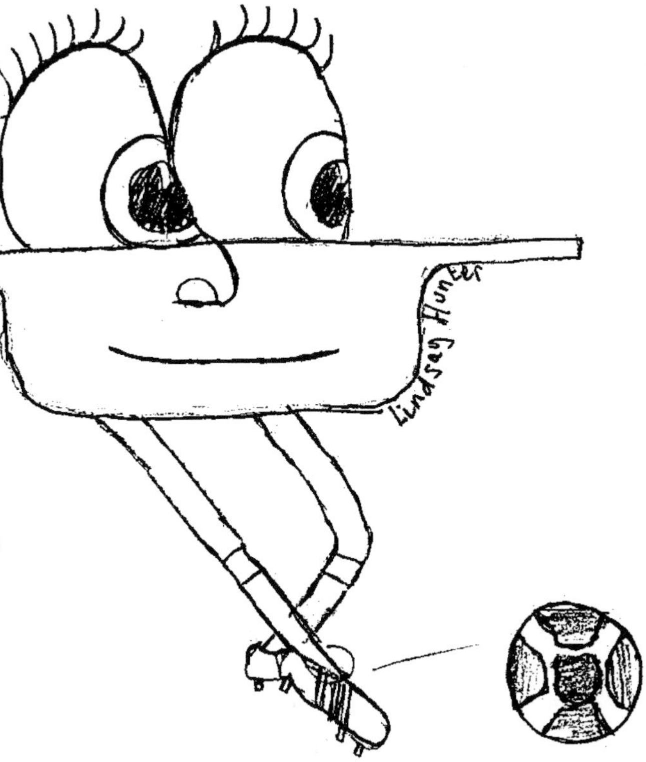

Ingredients:
5 fluid ounces of Gazza Tears
one packet of Salt and Linneker
  crisps (for crusty top)
1/2 pint of Cantona gravy for Gallic
  flavouring and to add some kick
1 lb of Linneker sausages
10 butter fingers (David Seaman brand)
Plant 4 lb of Celtic potatoes (so they have
  something to lift this year)
2 ounces of Best Flower of Scotland
5 ounces of Rangers Blue Cheese
1 ounce of Celtic Green Cheese
a sprinkling of Coleman balls

This recipe should only be tackled on a Saturday to ensure the best results. Pass all the ingredients into a red hot cauldron (any football stadium); mix together in any formation and stir until the cooker shows the red card. Serve in pair of Gazza football boots for added flavour.

Sue Lawley

My Husband's Sunday Roast

I would like to share with you a culinary creation of my husband's. The scene is a South London Sunday on which work has kept me at my desk for too long to begin preparing a traditional roast. Husband disappears to kitchen to "knock something up" from a fairly ordinarily stocked larder and fridge. Less than an hour later, the result is a delicious surprise. This is what he did:

Roast one small corn-fed M&S chicken in butter for 50 minutes. Chop and cook mushrooms in butter in frying pan. Keep warm. Skin fresh tomatoes and add small amount of chilli, garlic and basil to make salsa. Chill.
Cook Uncle Ben's rice and, as you do, remove chicken from oven and wrap in foil to keep warm. Drain rice and, at last moment, tip into oven-proof dish in which you cooked chicken. Add mushrooms and finally juice which has drained from chicken (inside and out).

Serve on warm plates and have salsa and leafy, French-dressed salad separately. The mixture of hot and cold, spicy and herby, soft and crunchy is perfect.

N.B. I must work on a Sunday more often!

Dame Felicity Lott

New Orleans Daube of Beef

2 1/2–3 lb topside or round of beef in one piece
a dozen black olives
3/4 lb salt streaky pork or bacon
a large onion
4 or 5 tomatoes
bouquet of herbs (bay leaf, fresh parsley,
  sprigs of thyme, dried basil)
butter or dripping
1/2 teacup of rum
salt, pepper, garlic

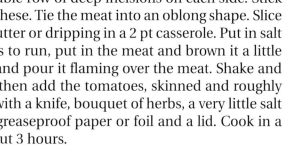

Trim excess fat from meat and make a double row of deep incisions on each side. Stick half an olive (cut lengthways) into each of these. Tie the meat into an oblong shape. Slice the onion and let it brown slightly in the butter or dripping in a 2 pt casserole. Put in salt pork, cut in pieces, and when the fat starts to run, put in the meat and brown it a little on each side. Heat the rum, set light to it and pour it flaming over the meat. Shake and rotate the pan until the flames die down, then add the tomatoes, skinned and roughly chopped, a clove or two of garlic crushed with a knife, bouquet of herbs, a very little salt and lots of pepper. Cover with a sheet of greaseproof paper or foil and a lid. Cook in a very slow oven – gas Mark 1, 290°F, for about 3 hours.

Remove bouquet before serving and crush the tomatoes into the sauce with a wooden spoon. Best served with rice or new potatoes and a salad.

Lovely rich sauce, and you can't really identify the nature of the alcohol!

Mrs. John Major

Mexican Chicken

(serves 4)

8 chicken thighs
3 tbsp flour
1 tsp salt
1 tsp paprika
1/4 tsp black pepper
2 oz butter
2 tbsp oil
1 onion, chopped

3 tbsp lemon juice
2 tbsp Worcester sauce
2 tbsp Tabasco
1/2 pt water
1/4 pt tomato ketchup
1 tsp sugar
1 tsp chilli powder
1/4 tsp oregano

Shake chicken in flour, salt, paprika and black pepper.
Brown chicken in foaming butter and oil.
Place in baking dish.
Add onion to oil and butter and cook until soft.
Add all remaining ingredients and cook
for 10 minutes over a gentle heat.
Pour mixture over chicken,
cover and bake in a moderate oven
until tender, keeping well basted.

Serve with rice and green salad.

Geoffrey Palmer

My family and I have spent many holidays in Tuscany and Umbria and this is why I like this particular recipe.

Pasta with Tuscan Chicken Sauce

(serves 6)

Ingredients:

1 lb tagliatelle verde	1 onion	1/4 pt double cream
6 oz raw chicken	freshly ground black pepper	1 green pepper
1 bunch parsley	2 tbsp olive oil	1 clove garlic
4 oz streaky bacon	1 tin beef consommé	salt

Method:
1. Remove seeds from pepper and roughly chop flesh.
2. Bring consommé to boil and reduce by half.
3. Add cream and continue to boil until reduced by half.
4. Season with salt and pepper.
5. Process the parsley (having already removed the coarse stalks) in a food processor (if not, chop).
6. Process the roughly chopped onion and garlic with the rindless, roughly chopped bacon and remove.
7. Process the green pepper until finely chopped and remove.
8. Process the cubed chicken until coarsely chopped.
9. Heat oil in a frying pan, add bacon, onion and garlic and cook over low heat until the onion is soft.
10. Add the chicken and green pepper and continue to cook on a medium heat until the chicken is tender. Season.
11. Cook tagliatelle until tender.
12. Add chicken mixture and toss well.
13. Add hot consommé sauce and parsley and toss well.

Susan and Lester Piggott

Cheese Soufflé

(serves 2)

SOUFFLE

Charlotte Watt

Ingredients:

1 1/2 oz flour	4 egg whites	1 1/2 oz butter
1/2 pt milk	3 egg yolks	3 oz cheese
salt, pepper and mustard		

Method:

Melt butter, and stir in flour. Add milk gradually, stirring and allowing mixture to thicken, then add seasoning. Grate cheese and combine with mixture. Remove from heat, beat egg yolks and add. Whisk egg whites until very stiff, and fold into mixture. Pour into a soufflé dish, and bake for 35 minutes in a moderate oven (350°F or 4/5 gas). Serve with a green salad.

Nick Nairn
Braeval Restaurant
By Aberfoyle
Stirling

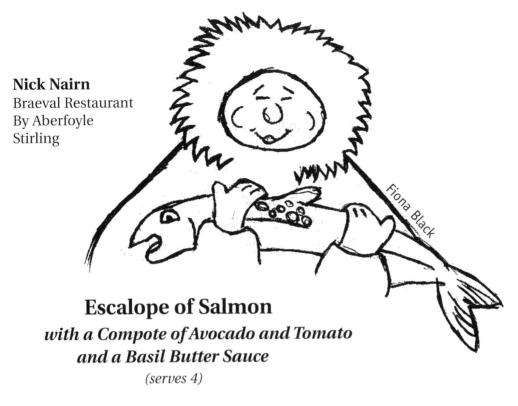

Fiona Black

Escalope of Salmon
with a Compote of Avocado and Tomato and a Basil Butter Sauce

(serves 4)

4 x 3 oz salmon escalopes
peanut oil

Sauce: 18 fl oz of Nage/vegetable stock
5 oz unsalted butter
18 leaves picked fresh basil
lemon juice and seasoning

Avocado Compote: 1 large ripe avocado (preferably with crinkly skin)
2 ripe plum tomatoes
juice of a lime
1 tbsp extra virgin olive oil
dash of both Worcester sauce and tabasco

Sauce: Reduce Nage to 4 fl oz and whisk in cold diced butter using a Braun wand/stick liquidiser (or similar). Season mixture and keep warm. Add chopped basil at the last minute.

Compote: Skin avocado and chop into smallish dice. Skin and quarter tomatoes, remove seeds and chop into concasse. Add oil to the mixture of avocado and tomato along with lime juice, Worcester sauce, tabasco and seasoning.

Salmon: Quickly fry salmon in peanut oil in a hot pan on best side only for approximately 2 minutes until crisp – fish should have a seared appearance, dark at edges. Remove from pan and place uncooked side down, squeeze lemon juice over and season with Maldon salt and black pepper.

To serve: Place a dollop of compote in centre of plate. Pour sauce over and around compote, then place escalope on top.

Lord Oaksey

Favos Gisados

(first course or supper for 6 people)

1 1/2 lb broad beans (young)
2 smoked gammon steaks
1 medium onion

1 glass dry white wine
stock to cover
oil

Cut gammon into diced pieces. Chop onion. Fry the onion with the gammon in a little oil until cooked (but not brown). Add beans with enough stock and wine to cover and simmer gently with a lid on until beans are tender (about 5–7 minutes).
Leave to stand off heat (still covered) for beans to take up flavour of gammon.
Reheat and season when ready to serve – may not need salt as gammon quite salty.
Can be made hours before needed.

Lord Palumbo
(This recipe was very kindly given to us by Lady Palumbo.)

Lentil Salad

8 oz brown lentils
1 tsp salt
1 clove garlic
3 tsp lemon juice
4 tsp olive oil
1/2 tsp cumin (in powder)
2 tsp finely chopped parsley
1 bunch of spring onions and pitta bread, to serve.

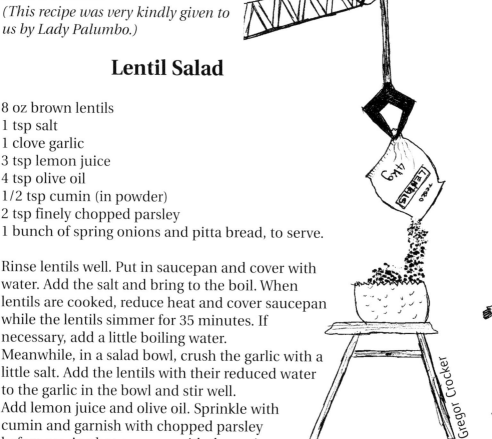

Rinse lentils well. Put in saucepan and cover with water. Add the salt and bring to the boil. When lentils are cooked, reduce heat and cover saucepan while the lentils simmer for 35 minutes. If necessary, add a little boiling water.
Meanwhile, in a salad bowl, crush the garlic with a little salt. Add the lentils with their reduced water to the garlic in the bowl and stir well.
Add lemon juice and olive oil. Sprinkle with cumin and garnish with chopped parsley before serving hot or warm with the spring onions and pitta bread.

Rosamunde Pilcher

Peg Bracken's Hootenholler Whisky Cake

A good gambit, with Potluck under discussion, is to move in fast with the dessert. You say, "Girls, I'll bring my wonderful Hootenholler Whisky Cake." (These things must always be done with a good show of enthusiasm.) Suggesting this cake is shrewd, too, because you can make it six months ago, it's easy and very good, it's cheap, as good cakes go, and as good cakes go, it goes a long way. Also, it has a rakish sound which is rather intriguing.

Ingredients:

1/2 cup butter
1 cup sugar
3 beaten eggs
1 cup flour
1/2 tsp baking powder
pinch of salt
1/2 tsp nutmeg
1/4 cup milk
1/4 cup black treacle
1/4 tsp baking soda
1 lb seedless raisins
2 cups chopped pecans or
    walnuts
1/4 cup whisky

Kerrie-Lee Mathews

Method:

First, take the whisky out of the cupboard and have a small snort for medicinal purposes. Now, cream the butter with the sugar and add the beaten eggs. Mix together the flour, baking powder, salt and nutmeg and add it to the butter mixture. Then add the milk. Now, put the soda into the treacle and mix it up and add that. Then add the raisins, nuts and whisky. Pour into a greased and floured loaf tin and bake at 300 °F for 2 hours.

Your whisky cake keeps practically forever, wrapped in aluminium foil and then put into a tin. It gets better and better, too, if you buck it up once in a while, by stabbing it with an ice pick and injecting a little more whisky with an eye dropper.

Ronnie Corbett

Grilled Salmon with Sauce Verte

(serves 4)

To cook salmon in this way, with the skin intact, produces a marvellous crust with the flesh of the fish being just cooked. The accompanying sauce is aromatic and mayonnaise-like in consistency. You will need a stove-top cast-iron ribbed grill for this dish.

700 g / 1 lb 8 oz piece of boned fillet of salmon
    scaled but not skinned, cut into 4 pieces
a little olive oil
1 tsp sea salt
pepper

For the sauce:
a bunch of flat-leaf parsley, leaves only
a bunch of watercress, leaves only
4 sprigs of tarragon, leaves only
4 sprigs of mint, leaves only
10 basil leaves
2 anchovy fillets
1 quantity aioli (see below)
green salad to serve

Aioli:
2 egg yolks
1 large garlic clove, peeled and crushed
salt and pepper
300–450 ml / 1/2–3/4 pt olive oil
juice of 1 lemon

Stephanie Miller

Method:
To make the aioli, first make sure all the ingredients are at room temperature. Traditionally aioli should be made in a pestle and mortar, but, failing that, a bowl and a whisk, or an electric mixer, will do. Do not use a blender or whole eggs. Beat together the egg yolks and the garlic with a little salt until thick. Start to add the olive oil in a thin stream, beating continuously. Add a little of the lemon juice and then some more oil. Continue beating, adding alternately more lemon juice and more oil until both are used up and you have a thick mayonnaise. Adjust the salt and add plenty of pepper. Cover and keep at room temperature.

Preheat the grill. Bring a large pan of water to the boil, throw in the parsley and watercress leaves, give a quick stir and drain. Rinse briefly with cold water and squeeze dry in a tea towel. Chop the tarragon, mint and basil leaves with the anchovies until extremely fine. Do the same to the parsley and watercress, and stir all of them into the aioli. Check the seasoning and sharpen with a little extra lemon juice if necessary.

Brush the skin-side of the salmon with olive oil and sprinkle evenly with the sea salt. Grind pepper over the flesh side. Place on the grill, skin-side down, and cook for about 3–5 minutes, or until the skin is well crisped and almost blackened. Turn over and cook on the flesh side for about the same amount of time. Transfer to a hot plate and rest in a luke-warm oven for 5 minutes. Arrange on individual plates together with a green salad and a spoonful of the sauce verte. Serve with lemon wedges if you wish.

Angela Piper
Jennifer in *The Archers*

Based on a typical Danish dessert, Thorkil suggested this superb recipe to Pat Archer.

Bridge Farm Blackberry Butterscotch Cream
(serves 4)

2 large cooking apples	1 lb (450 g) freshly picked blackberries
3 tbsp clear honey	1/2 tsp cinnamon or 1/2 cinnamon stick
5 fl oz (150 ml/1/4 pt) double cream	5 fl oz (150 ml/1/4 pt) yogurt
For the topping:	4 oz (100 g) coarse white breadcrumbs
3 oz (75 g) unsalted butter	1 oz (25 g) caster sugar

Peel and slice the apples and put with the rinsed blackberries in a saucepan. Add the honey and cinnamon and simmer over a low heat until the fruit is soft. Remove the cinnamon stick, allow the fruit to cool a little and put into a glass bowl. Whip the cream, adding the yogurt spoonful by spoonful until thick. Keep to one side until the topping is made.

For the topping, melt the butter in a clean frying pan and add the breadcrumbs and sugar. Gently brown the breadcrumbs, stirring to prevent them from burning. When golden brown, spread out onto a large plate to cool. Sprinkle some of these crunchy crumbs onto the fruit.

Put the cream/yogurt mixture on top and the remaining crumbs as a final layer.

David Nicholls
Executive Chef, The Ritz Hotel, London

Suprême of Chicken with Roquefort
(4 covers)

1 head of celery	*Sauce:*
4 suprêmes of chicken	1 1/2 lb butter
1 lb roquefort cheese	1 tbsp double cream
2 golden delicious apples	1 tbsp sherry vinegar
1/2 lb sultanas	1 chopped shallot
	squeezed juice of half a lemon

Method: Trim suprêmes of all fat and sinew and remove wing knuckle. Make incision lengthways down the side and cut almost in half. Place suprêmes between sheets of clingfilm and lightly batten out to give a nice escalope. Soften the cheese and mould into 4 and place down centre of chicken. Take each breast and envelop the cheese. Place clingfilm once again and roll lightly to form a cylindrical shape. These are now ready to steam or lightly poach in water. Soak the sultanas in water. Peel and trim apples. Cut in slices (thick) and cut again into batons. Quickly cook in boiling water with dash of lemon juice. Refresh in iced water. Peel celery and trim to cut into batons the same size as apples and repeat cooking process.

For the sauce: Place vinegar, cream and chopped shallot into saucepan and reduce till cream thickens. Add a little butter at a time, boiling consistently. Adding more butter to the sauce, a little spot of water can be added, adjusting the thickness of the sauce. When all butter is added, season with salt and pepper and add lemon juice. Pass through strainer. Poach or steam chicken for approximately 12–15 minutes. Add celery, sultanas and apple to the butter sauce. Remove cooked chicken from clingfilm and cut into 4–5 nice slices. Spoon the sauce onto plate and arrange the slices of chicken around the centre. Garnish with flat parsley or chervil.

Kevin MacGillivray
Ballathie House Hotel, Kinclaven, Perthshire

Breast of Pheasant filled with a Mushroom and Tarragon Farce
served with its own Sausage on a Green Lentil Sauce *(serves 2)*

1 x 2 lb pheasant and livers	1 egg yolk
10g chopped fresh herbs – tarragon, parsley, thyme	160 ml double cream
50g chopped mixed wild mushrooms	1 tbsp olive oil
1 pinch nutmeg	20g cooked green lentils
100g finely diced root vegetables	2 measures of Madeira
sausage skins (available from butcher)	onion, carrot, celery

Remove the legs from the pheasant and take off all the meat. Reserve 30g. Liquidise the remainder with the egg yolk and set over ice. Slowly work in the cream and season with salt, pepper and nutmeg. Sauté the mushrooms, drain and cool.

Kevin MacGillivray's *Breast of Pheasant continued*

Dice the livers and mix with the reserved 30g pheasant meat and the finely diced vegetables. Fill into the sausage skins.

Combine the cooked mushrooms with the mousse, add the chopped herbs and place in a piping bag ready for use. Remove the wishbone from the pheasant, then remove the suprêmes. Make an incision into the suprême and fill with the mushroom farce until plump. Chop the carcass for the sauce. Heat the olive oil in a pan, add the chopped bones and trimmings with some onion, carrot and celery. Deglaze with Madeira and cover with water. Simmer for 45 minutes. Strain and reduce until consistency is reached, add the lentils and check for seasoning.

To serve, poach the sausages gently in water for 4–6 minutes. Brush the pheasant breasts with olive oil and place in a hot oven, over 375°F for around 15 minutes. When cooked, rest for 5 minutes, then carve onto heated plates and serve with the lentil sauce.

Angela Piper
Jennifer in *The Archers*

Home Farm Venison and Pheasant Casserole

This rich casserole can serve up to 6 people depending on the size of the pheasants and people's appetites.

2 lb (1 kg) haunch of venison, sliced and
  cut into bite-sized cubes
3 pheasant breasts, sliced into slivers
1 bottle red wine
1 plump garlic clove, crushed

2 large onions, chopped
sprig of sage, chopped
1 tsp honey mustard
olive oil for frying

For the marinade:
2 tbsp juniper berries, crushed

3 tbsp olive oil
salt and pepper

rind and juice of 2 oranges
4 garlic cloves, crushed

Mix together all the ingredients for the marinade, adding half the bottle of red wine. Place in 2 covered bowls and marinate the venison and pheasant separately overnight. Remove the venison and pheasant from the marinade, pat dry on absorbent kitchen roll and keep separate. Strain and reserve the marinade. In a large frying pan heat 1 tbsp of olive oil and quickly fry the venison until browned on all sides. Remove to an ovenproof casserole.

Fry the pheasant breast slices in the pan over a fairly high heat until just browned on both sides, then remove to a separate dish. Add a little more oil to the pan and fry the onions and garlic for about a minute. Transfer to the casserole containing the venison. Add the sage, the remainder of the bottle of wine and the reserved marinade to the casserole. Stir in the honey mustard and season. Place in a moderate oven at 325°F/160°C/Gas 3 and cook for 1 hour, then add the pheasant breasts. Continue cooking for another hour or until the meat is tender. Pour the casserole juices into a saucepan, skim off the fat and boil briskly to thicken the sauce. Pour over the meat, cover and keep warm until ready to serve.

Magnus Magnusson

Lambasteik
(Roast Leg of Lamb)

Sprinkle a half or whole fresh leg of lamb rather generously with salt, pepper and garlic powder. Bake at 400°F for about 2 hours.

Just before serving, make gravy by adding hot water to the pan to deglaze it. Thicken with flour and water.

Lamb should be served as fast as possible. Serve with sugar-glazed potatoes, sweet and sour green tomatoes, a favourite jam, green peas and spicy cucumber salad.

© Margret Geppert, Leif Eiriksson, *Icelandic Club Cookbook*

Lord Menuhin

Salmon en Croûte
(for 4–6 people)

1 1/2 lb piece of salmon, divided into 2 long fillets	3 thin gammon rashers
1 lb asparagus, cooked	8 oz prepared puff pastry
2 tbsp double cream	1 egg yolk
1/2 tsp dill, chopped	1 tbsp milk
salt and black pepper	

Cut off the soft tips of the cooked asparagus and rub through a coarse sieve or liquidise. Blend the cream and dill into this asparagus purée and season to taste. Spread the asparagus purée over one of the prepared fish fillets and put the fish together.

Wrap the gammon slices round the salmon and leave on one side.

Roll out the pastry on a floured surface to a rectangle about 10 in x 12 in. Place the salmon on the pastry and wrap the pastry over the fish. Brush the edges of the pastry with the lightly beaten egg yolk mixed with the milk. Tuck in all edges and seal with egg. Place the salmon upside down on a wet baking tray, decorating the top with pastry leftovers. Cut a couple of holes in the pastry to allow the steam to escape. Brush with the remaining egg and milk.

Bake in the centre of a pre-heated oven at 425°F for 20 minutes, then lower the heat to 375°F and bake for a further 20–25 minutes or until the pastry is golden brown.

Serve with new potatoes tossed in butter and dill and a cucumber salad.

Spike Milligan

Spaghetti Dolce
(for 4 people)

spaghetti, cooked al dente, no salt, for about 8 minutes
5 oz carton double cream
2 tbsp brandy
castor sugar to taste

Cook spaghetti. Whilst this is cooking, mix together cream, brandy and castor sugar. When spaghetti is ready, pour over the cream.

Dame Vera Lynn

Turkey Boobs
(for 2 people)

Cook in frying pan with lid.

2 turkey breasts
2 sliced onions
2–3 chopped tomatoes
garlic
stock

Lightly sauté onions in small amount of fat of your choice with chopped garlic cloves (according to taste). Place turkey breasts on top, with a small amount of stock. Simmer gently with lid on. Prepare 2–3 skinned tomatoes and finely chop. Add tomatoes to frying pan with a little salt and pepper and simmer until turkey is completely cooked through.

As I never use recipes I add various herbs and/or spices that I may have at hand, such as lemon juice, ginger, dried or fresh herbs, lovage, thyme, fenugreek, etc. One can also use leeks instead of onions. Serve with brown rice and salad or vegetables.

Diane Modahl

Norwegian Meat Balls

(serves 4)

This is a typical Friday meal in Norway – meat balls in brown cream sauce.

500g beef mince
3–4 slices of white bread
1 tsp milk
1 oz flour
2 tbsp butter

salt and ground black pepper to taste
1 pt cream
1/2 pt red wine
1/2 pt beef stock

Prepare bread by removing crusts and making the remainder into breadcrumbs.
Melt butter and pour over beef, breadcrumbs and flour. Mix thoroughly by hand and shape into balls. Place in oven-proof dish and cook in oven at 180°C for 40–50 minutes.
Prepare sauce by boiling cream, red wine and beef stock.
Add meat balls when sauce has thickened and leave simmering on low heat for 10–15 minutes.

Christopher Martin-Jenkins

Haddock Mayonnaise

(serves 6)

Patrick Murphy

A starter or main course for the cricket season.

2 lb smoked haddock fillet
1 cucumber
1 chopped hard-boiled egg
salt and pepper
6 tbs fromage frais
parsley
6 tbs Hellmans or home-made mayonnaise

Pour boiling water over the smoked haddock, cover and leave to cool. Drain the haddock, skin and flake it and mix with the egg, fromage frais and mayonnaise. Season.
Divide the peeled cucumber in half. Dice one half and fold it into the fish mixture. Slice the other half very thinly for decoration.
Pile the haddock mixture on to a flat serving plate and surround it with a ring of overlapping cucumber slices.
Decorate the fish with parsley.
Serve with new potatoes and salad.

Peter Scudamore

Roast Duckling and Orange Sauce

(for 4 people)

Roast Duckling
Prick the skin of the duckling all over and rub with salt. Roast in a hot oven (approximately 200°C) for required amount of time. Allow 25 minutes per lb.

Sauce
1 level tbsp flour
Coarsely grated peel and juice of 2 medium oranges
2 tbsp dry red wine
2 level tbsp redcurrant jelly
half wine glass dry sherry
seasoning to taste

Pour fat and juices from tin into a saucepan over low heat and stir in flour. After 1 minute add the other sauce ingredients and stir to combine. Allow to simmer. Garnish with 2 thinly sliced and peeled oranges and watercress.

Drawing done for
Linda McCartney's
Vegetable Spring Rolls
by
Karen Still

Linda McCartney

Vegetable Spring Rolls

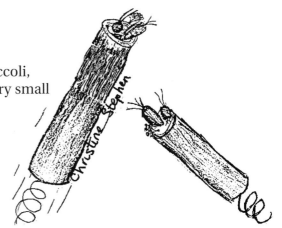

2 tbsp groundnut or olive oil + for deep frying
12 oz mixed vegetables (eg. mangetout, peas, broccoli,
    courgettes, carrots, water-chestnuts), all cut very small
5 oz button mushrooms, chopped
3 oz beansprouts
4 spring onions, chopped finely
2 inches root ginger, peeled and grated
1 clove garlic
2–3 tbsp soy sauce
24 sheets of filo pastry

Heat the groundnut oil and stir fry all the prepared vegetables with the ginger and garlic. Stir in soy sauce to taste. Remove from the heat, cover and leave to stand for several minutes.

Put 2 tablespoons of the vegetable filling on a single filo sheet and roll it up, tucking in the sides to make a neat parcel. Immediately roll this roll in another sheet of filo. Repeat to make 12 spring rolls in all. Deep fry in very hot oil (190°C / 375°F), turning the spring rolls until they are light golden all over and crisp. Drain on kitchen paper and serve as soon as possible with sweet and sour sauce.

Sweet and Sour Sauce

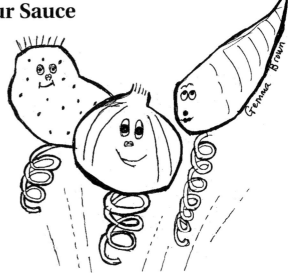

1/4 pt pineapple juice
3 tbsp olive oil
3 tbsp light soft brown sugar
1 tbsp soy sauce, more to taste
1 inch root ginger, peeled and finely grated
2 cloves garlic, crushed
4 tbsp fresh lemon juice
1 heaped tbsp cornflour
freshly ground black pepper

Combine the pineapple juice, oil, sugar, soy sauce, ginger, garlic and 2 tbsp of the lemon juice in a saucepan. Heat until the sugar dissolves. Mix the cornflour with the remaining lemon juice, add to the pan and stir until the sauce is smooth and thick. Season with pepper. Simmer very gently for 5 minutes, stirring occasionally.

Anton Mosimann

Steamed Fillet of Sea Bass Oriental

(serves 4)

4 sea bass fillets, 150g/5oz each
100ml/3 1/2fl oz fish stock
1 1/2 tsp soy sauce
100g/4oz woodear mushrooms,
    soaked and drained
50g/2oz lilli flower mushrooms,
    soaked and drained
2 tbsp sesame oil
150g/5oz each yellow and green courgette,
    sliced at an angle
100g/4oz fennel, thinly sliced
25g/1oz tomato concasse (skinned, seeded and roughly chopped tomatoes)
seasoning
1 tbsp snipped chives and coriander sprigs, to garnish

Sarah Herbert

1. Season the fillets, steam for 3–5 minutes. Keep warm.
2. Heat the fish stock and soy sauce, add the mushrooms and bring to the boil. Cook gently for 3–4 minutes. Season. Remove from the heat and keep warm.
3. Heat the oil in a frying pan, add the courgettes and fennel and quickly sauté to soften. Add the tomatoes and seasoning and cook for a few seconds.
4. To serve, spoon the vegetables in the middle of each plate and lay a sea bass fillet on top. Cover with the mushrooms and drizzle over a little of the mushroom cooking liquor and garnish.

Stirling Moss

Tuna or Salmon Mousse

1 can condensed tomato soup
1 (8 oz) packet of cream cheese
1 cup diced green pepper
1 cup diced celery
1 small grated onion

1 cup mayonnaise
1 large can tuna or salmon (remove skin
    and bones)
2 tablespoons unflavoured gelatine
1/2 cup cold water

Method:
Melt in a double boiler the tomato soup and cream cheese. When cooled, put in green pepper, diced celery, grated onion, mayonnaise and fish. (For a smoother mousse, combine cooled mixture with mayonnaise and fish in a blender or Magimix before adding vegetables.)

Then add gelatine which has been dissolved in 1/2 cup cold water. Pour into oiled fish or other mould and chill until set.

Jackie Stewart

Roast Chicken with Almonds and Honey
(4–6 helpings)

Derek Anderson

1 chicken (for roasting)
1/2 lemon
pepper and salt
3 x 15 ml spoons honey
50 g blanched sliced almonds
pinch of powdered saffron (optional)
2 x 15 ml spoons oil

Truss the chicken and rub with lemon. Salt and sprinkle with pepper. Line a roasting tin with a piece of foil large enough to cover the bird completely. Put the bird on the foil and rub all over with honey. Sprinkle the almonds and saffron (optional) over the bird, then cover gently with oil. Wrap it completely, keeping foil away from the skin. Fold over the edges to seal. Roast in a moderate/fairly hot oven, 180°C – 190°C for about 1 1/2 hours until tender. Uncover the bird for the last 10 minutes to allow for browning.

Albert Roux
Le Gavroche
43 Upper Brook Street
London

Cassoulet de Castelnaudary

(serves 8-10)

The origins of cassoulet are uncertain; it is found all over Languedoc, including Toulouse, Carcassonne and Castelnaudary. The garnishes vary slightly and partridge is sometimes used instead of lamb. Our own undisputed favourite is the one we have given you here, made with pork and lamb.

Preparation time:	20 minutes, plus soaking the beans
Cooking time:	3 3/4 hours
Equipment:	1 large round copper or glazed earthenware casserole
	Mincing machine or food processor

Ingredients:

1.2 kg / 2 3/4 lb small dried white haricot beans
1 unsmoked boiling sausage (about 250 g / 9 oz)
4 coarse Toulouse sausages
400 g / 14 oz salt belly of pork
1 semi-salted knuckle of pork
300 g / 11 oz fresh pork rind, rolled and tied into a sausage shape
200 g / 7 oz carrots, peeled
200 g / 7 oz onions, peeled and halved, 1 half stuck with 2 cloves
1 large bouquet garni
4 garlic cloves
10 peppercorns, crushed
shoulder of lamb (about 1 kg / 2lb 3 oz)
2 tablespoons goose fat or lard
300 g / 11 oz ripe tomatoes, peeled, deseeded and chopped
30 g / 1 oz chopped parsley
60 g / 2 oz dried white breadcrumbs
2 preserved goose legs, home-made or tinned
salt

Preparation

The beans: Soak overnight in cold water.

The sausages and meats: Prick the sausages with the point of a knife and place them in a large saucepan with the belly and knuckle of pork. Cover with cold water and bring to the boil to blanch them. As soon as the water boils, lift out all the sausages with a slotted spoon and put them in a pan of cold water. Leave the pieces of pork to cook gently for 3 minutes, then refresh them in cold water. Drain the pork and sausages.

Cooking the Cassoulet

Drain the beans and put them in the casserole. Cover with plenty of cold, unsalted water. Add the whole peeled carrots, the onions, bouquet garni, 3 halved garlic cloves and the peppercorns. Bring to the boil, then lower the heat and simmer very gently, skimming the surface as necessary. After 20 minutes, put in the knuckle of pork and the pork rind.

The shoulder of lamb: Bone the lamb and cut away the sinews and fat, then cut the meat into 8 pieces of even weight. Heat the goose fat or lard in a frying pan and quickly brown the pieces of lamb, then drain them in a colander.

The tomatoes: When the beans have been cooking for 1 hour, add the belly of pork and the chopped tomatoes. The beans must be kept covered with liquid; add a little boiling water if necessary.

The lamb and boiling sausage: When the cassoulet has been cooking for 1 1/2 hours, put in the lamb and boiling sausage to cook, skimming the surface from time to time. A glorious smell of cassoulet should start to waft out.

The Toulouse sausages: After another hour, grill the sausages just to brown the surface and add them to the casserole. Simmer the cassoulet for a further 30 minutes.

Final cooking and serving

Preheat the oven to 150°C / 300°F / gas 2.

After 3 hours cooking, the beans will be deliciously melting, the meats well cooked and succulent. Taste the beans to see whether they need salt; since the pork and sausages are already salty, this may not be necessary. Discard the bouquet garni, carrots and onions.

Mince or process the pork rind to a purée and, using a spatula, mix in the parsley and breadcrumbs.

Roll the remaining garlic clove in salt and rub it over the bottom of 2 deep serving plates. Pile in the lamb and beans. Slice the belly and knuckle of pork, following the line of the bone, then cut the meat into chunks and mix it with the lamb and beans.

Remove the skins from the sausages and slice them. Arrange them on top of the dish. Shred the goose legs and push the pieces into the middle of the cassoulet. Finally, spread the breadcrumb mixture evenly over the top and cook in the preheated oven for 45 minutes, during which time a lovely crust will form. If you like, you can break up this crust with a fork and return the cassoulet to the oven so that a second crust forms. Place the dish under a salamander or a hot grill to brown the crust.

Presentation

Serve the cassoulet straight from the dish. Between the first and second helpings, serve a salad of frisée with garlic croûtons. We like to eat a cassoulet this way, accompanied by a good red Cahors or a mature Corbières.

Note: This dish can be successfully reheated and may actually taste better.

Alison Price

Roast Halibut, Crispy Leek and Mushroom Risotto with Sauce Vierge

(serves 6)

Ingredients:
6 oz fillet of halibut, skinned, per person
  (N.B. try to choose the halibut from a medium-sized fish so that the portion is square and thick rather than long and thin.)
2 leeks

Sauce Vierge:
6 tomatoes, skinned, seeded and diced
2 teaspoons crushed coriander seeds
20 leaves fresh chopped basil
30ml lemon juice

3 finely chopped shallots
1 clove finely chopped garlic
300ml red wine
500ml virgin olive oil

Risotto:
600g wild mushrooms
3 garlic cloves peeled and sliced
sea salt and freshly ground black pepper
2 tablespoons chopped fresh herbs
4 shallots finely chopped
175g finely grated fresh parmesan

7 tablespoons olive oil
juice of 1 lemon
1 litre chicken stock
150g butter
300g risotto rice
75ml white wine

Method:
Leeks: Cut the leeks into very fine strips about 5cm long and deep fry at about 180°C. Remove before they get dark and bitter and drain onto a paper towel.
Season with salt and pepper.

Sauce Vierge: Heat a small amount of oil in a small pan, add the shallots, garlic and coriander seeds and allow to sweat.
Add the red wine and reduce until almost dry.
Add the lemon juice and the rest of the olive oil and gently heat.
Add the basil and allow to infuse for a few moments, then add the tomato dice and serve immediately.

Risotto: In a heavy-bottomed frying pan sauté mushrooms in 4 tablespoons of olive oil, season with salt, pepper and lemon juice. Place in a colander and collect the juices.
Heat the chicken stock.
Melt 75g of the butter and 3 tablespoons of the olive oil in a large heavy-bottomed deep pan and sauté the shallots and garlic. Add salt and pepper to taste.

Add the rice and sweat for a moment – deglaze with white wine until syrupy.
Return to the heat, add the remaining mushroom juices and two ladlefuls of hot stock or just enough to cover the rice, and simmer, stirring, until the rice has absorbed all the liquid. Continue to add more stock as the previous addition is absorbed.

After about 15–20 minutes, nearly all of the stock will have been absorbed by the rice; each grain will have a creamy coating but will remain al dente.
Add the remaining butter in small pieces, the mushrooms and parmesan, being careful not to overstir. Serve immediately.

To assemble the dish: Pan fry your seasoned halibut until golden brown on one side – turn over to seal – finish cooking in the oven at 180° for maybe 10-12 minutes.
Place the cooked risotto in the centre of the plate, halibut on top completed with a neat pile of deep fried leeks.

Scatter your sauce vierge around the plate.
You may wish to serve baby leeks or roasted carrot with the halibut.

Geoffrey Boycott

Sour Cream Scones

1 lb 2 oz self raising flour
2 oz castor sugar
5 oz carton sour cream
7 oz butter
2 eggs
sultanas or raisins to taste (a good
   handful)
milk

Samantha Taylor

Sieve flour. Rub in butter, sugar and fruit.
Lightly beat eggs and fold into mixture gradually with sour cream and enough milk to make a soft dough. Turn onto floured board, roll lightly to 1/2–3/4" thick, cut into diamonds using palette knife, and bake on a tray in a hot oven at 220°C for 10–15 minutes.

Edward Stourton

Roast Lamb for Incompetent Male Show-Offs

Yvonne Bloice

Buy an expensive American barbecue with a domed lid.

Buy an outrageously expensive leg of lamb which cannot fail to taste good, some red wine, garlic and marmalade.

Find two old bricks.

Stuff sticks of garlic into the lamb with a knife – many more than you would imagine would be necessary.

Construct a large basin of silver foil for the lamb and place it in a baking tray. Pour at least half the wine bottle into the basin. Smear the lamb thickly with marmalade and then place it in the basin to marinade.

Light far too much charcoal in the barbecue and, when it has turned white hot, clear a space for the two bricks in the centre – if you use your hands to do this, you should drink the rest of the wine to dull the pain while waiting for the ambulance. Place the baking tray on the bricks, and close the top of the silver foil basin over the lamb so that the wine will boil and steam inside. Put the top on the barbecue so that it cooks like an oven.

Re-open the basin ten minutes before serving, so that the marmalade blackens.

The garlic and wine will ensure the result is delicious – the marmalade will earn the chef a reputation – in my case quite unjustified – for originality. The quantities and timings must be decided entirely by instinct – frequent thoughtful prodding adds to the social impact but can ruin the taste if overdone.

Michael Palin

Oxygen Tart

Ingredients: Pastry

Roll the pastry, make into a base, and top with nothing at all.
For special occasions, walnuts may be added, turning it into oxygen and walnut tart.

Rick Stein
The Seafood Restaurant
Padstow
Cornwall

Thai Fish Cakes with Green Beans
(Tod Man Pla)
(serves 4)

450 g (1 lb) ling or coley fillets, skinned and cut into chunks
1 tablespoon Thai fish sauce (nam pla)
1 tablespoon red curry paste
1 kaffir lime leaf or 1 strip of lime zest, very finely shredded
1 tablespoon chopped fresh coriander (leaves and stalks)
1 egg
1 teaspoon palm sugar or muscovado sugar
1/2 teaspoon salt
40 g (1 1/2 oz) French beans, thinly sliced into rounds
150 ml (5 fl oz) groundnut or sunflower oil

For the sweet and sour cucumber sauce:
50 ml (2 fl oz) white wine vinegar
100 g (4 oz) caster sugar
1 1/2 tablespoons water
2 teaspoons Thai fish sauce (nam pla)
50 g (2 oz) cucumber, very finely diced
25 g (1 oz) carrot, very finely diced
25g (1oz) onion, very finely chopped
2 red birdseye chillies, thinly sliced

Charlotte Collard

Method:
For the sauce, gently heat the vinegar, sugar and water in a small pan until the sugar has dissolved. Bring to the boil and boil for 1 minute, then remove from the heat and leave to cool. Stir in the fish sauce, cucumber, carrot, onion and chillies. Pour into 4 small dipping saucers or ramekins and set aside.

For the fish cakes, put the fish in a food processor with the fish sauce, curry paste, kaffir lime leaf or lime zest, chopped coriander, egg, sugar and salt. Process until smooth, then stir in the sliced green beans.

Divide the mixture into 16 pieces. Roll each one into a ball and then flatten into a 6 cm (2 1/2 in) disc. Heat the oil in a large frying pan and fry the fish cakes in batches for 1 minute on each side, until golden brown. Lift out and drain on kitchen paper, then serve with the sweet and sour cucumber sauce.

Brian Turner
Turner's
Walton Street, London

Roast Top Rump of Beef
Roast Vegetables, Yorkshire Pudding, Gravy and Horseradish Sauce
(serves 4)

Ingredients:
2–2 1/2 lb top rump of beef
1 lb carrots
1 lb parsnips
1 lb potatoes
dripping
1/2 pt gravy
salt and pepper

Yorkshire pudding:
2 eggs
5–6 oz flour
1/4 pt water
1/4 pt milk
salt
dripping

Jason Pooley

Method:
Peel and trim the vegetables and cut into quarters 3" long.

Seal the meat in dripping in a hot roasting tray. Colour very strongly.
Put into hot oven – 220°C for about 45–50 minutes. After 15 minutes of cooking the beef, slightly colour the vegetables in a frying pan with dripping.

Tip the vegetables into the roasting tray around the beef – season the beef and the vegetables at this point. Finish cooking the meat to the desired point of doneness.
Take the beef out and leave to rest for 10 minutes.

When ready to serve, warm up the vegetables and beef. Slice the beef, place the vegetables and then beef on the plate. Take Yorkshire puddings from oven and put on plate. Serve with gravy and horseradish sauce.

To prepare Yorkshire puddings:
Break eggs into bowl and lightly mix. Add half the water and milk, all the flour and 1 tsp salt. Mix to a smooth paste. Add the rest of the liquor and allow to rest for 2–3 hours if possible. Put your Yorkshire pud tins into oven with dripping and allow to get very hot.

Pour in the mix and cook at about 250°C for approximately 20 minutes until cooked. Serve immediately.

Gordon Ramsay
Aubergine
11, Park Walk
London

Roast Rump of Lamb Niçoise

(serves 4)

For this dish you'll need chumps of steaks of lamb taken from the top of the leg where it joins the end of the saddle. Remove the little nut of bone and trim it of fat into a neat shape. Marinate this dish at least a day in advance for the best flavour and prepare the niçoise vegetables ahead.

4 chumps of lamb about 200 g (7 oz) each
extra virgin olive oil to marinate
4 sprigs each fresh thyme and rosemary
1 tablespoon coriander seeds, crushed
100 g (3 1/2 oz) black olives, stoned
150 g (5 1/2 oz) green olives, stoned
2 garlic cloves, crushed
1 tablespoon olive oil
2 small tian of aubergine
400 g (14 oz) tomatoes
200 g (7 oz) courgettes, thinly sliced
600 g (21 oz) baby new potatoes, preferably Jersey Royal
25 g (1 oz) butter, preferably clarified
100 ml lamb stock
salt and freshly ground black pepper

First place the lamb chumps in a dish and trickle over olive oil to just cover. Rub in well and place the herb sprigs and coriander seeds on top. Cover with cling film and leave to marinate in the fridge for about 24 hours if possible.

Finely chop the olives into fine dice and set aside, then deal with the garlic. If you do not have garlic comfit made up, sauté the crushed garlic cloves gently in the olive oil for about 10 minutes until softened. Do not allow to burn or it could taste bitter.

Make the tian of aubergine and set aside. Skin, quarter and de-seed the tomatoes, then slice into petals.

Preheat the grill and cook the courgette slices until lightly charred on both sides.

Heat the clarified butter in a frying pan and lightly sauté the potatoes, shaking the pan occasionally until they are just cooked.

Preheat the oven to 220°C, 425°F, gas mark 7. Using a large heavy-based frying pan or cast iron gratin dish with an oven-proof handle (i.e. no plastic or wood), heat a little oil in the pan until really hot, then brown the lamb chumps on both sides, removing the herb sprigs beforehand.

Gordon Ramsay's *Roast Rump of Lamb Niçoise continued*

Place the meat pan in the oven and cook for about 8 minutes, turning the chumps once or twice during cooking. Set aside to rest whilst you finish preparing the niçoise garnish and sauce.

For the sauce, re-heat the lamb stock in a small saucepan and add the chopped black and green olives plus the herbs. Bring to the boil and keep at a gentle simmer.

Slice the lamb chumps finely into 10–12 very thin slices each and fan out on four warmed dinner plates.

Arrange the courgette slices and baby potatoes around the outside of the dish together with the aubergine and tomatoes, then spoon over the sauce to glaze the meat. Serve immediately.

Marie Christine Ridgway

Moroccan Lamb
(generous for 4)

1 1/2 lb boned cubed lamb, shoulder or leg
2 sliced green peppers
1 tsp grated ginger
strip of orange peel
2 tbsp lemon juice
seasoning

flour
1 chopped head fennel
2 pinches saffron
4oz chopped dried apricots
3/4 pt vegetable stock
2 sliced onions

Brown floured meat in oil, then fry onions, peppers and fennel. Place in casserole. Add ginger, orange peel and stock, and bring to simmering point. Add saffron. Cook slowly for 1 3/4 hours. Add lemon juice and apricots and cook for a further 15 minutes. Season to taste.

Chicken and Mushrooms
(generous for 4)

6 boneless chicken fillets
8 oz field mushrooms
1 tbsp lemon juice
  (or sherry if preferred)

2 oz butter
1 dsp flour

2 cloves garlic, finely chopped
1/2 pt double cream
watercress, to garnish

Cut fillets into three. *Gently* fry chicken strips in butter until cooked. Transfer to warm dish. Fry mushrooms and garlic until just soft. Sprinkle over flour and continue to cook for a couple of minutes. Pour in cream and lemon juice. Bring to boil and stir for three minutes. Pour over chicken. Garnish with watercress.

Both recipes are good with rice and salad.

Anthea Turner

Smoked Fish Pie

(serves 4 people)

This is a lovely creamy fish pie with a mashed potato topping and a golden crust of melted cheese. You can in fact use any combination of smoked fish – sometimes a couple of ounces of smoked salmon offcuts make an interesting addition.

1 1/2 lb smoked haddock (700 g)
4 kipper fillets, weighing a total 4–6 oz (110–175 g)
1 pint milk (570 ml)
4 oz butter (110 g)
1 bay leaf
2 oz flour (50 g)
2 hard-boiled eggs, roughly chopped
3 tablespoons fresh chopped parsley
1 tablespoon capers (optional)
1 tablespoon lemon juice
salt and freshly milled black pepper

For the topping:
2 lb fresh boiled potatoes (900 g)
2 oz butter (50 g)
4 tablespoons milk
freshly grated nutmeg
1 oz strong Cheddar cheese (25 g), grated

Pre-heat the oven to gas mark 6, 200°C, 400°F.

Anthea Turner's *Smoked Fish Pie continued*

Arrange fish in a baking tin, pour half the milk over it, add a few flecks of the butter and the bay leaf, then bake in the oven for 15–20 minutes. Pour off and reserve the cooking liquid, then remove the skin from the fish and flake the flesh into largish pieces.

Next make the sauce by melting the remaining butter in a saucepan, then stirring in the flour and gradually adding the fish liquid bit by bit, stirring well after each addition. When all the liquid is in, finish the sauce by gradually adding the remaining milk, seasoning with salt and pepper and simmering for 3–4 minutes.

William Carcary

Now mix the fish into the sauce, together with the hard-boiled eggs, parsley and capers, then taste to see if it needs any more seasoning, and stir in the lemon juice. Pour the mixture into a buttered baking dish (about 2 1/2 pints / 1.5 litre capacity).

Next prepare the topping. Cream the potatoes, starting off with a large fork, then finishing off with an electric beater if you have one, adding the butter and milk. Season the potatoes with salt and pepper and add some freshly grated nutmeg. Spread evenly all over the fish, then sprinkle the cheese all over. Bake on a high shelf in the oven – still at gas mark 6, 200°C, 400°F – for about 30 minutes, by which time the pie will be heated through and the top will be nicely tinged with brown.

Bryn Terfel

Welsh Stew

Beef - potatoes - few carrots - onions - a small swede (if liked) - small pieces of home-cured bacon (if liked)

Cut up the meat into small pieces and place in a saucepan with the bacon and less cold water than you would use for soup. Simmer for about one hour before adding carrots, onions, swede (all cut up small), and continue to simmer for 1/2 hour. Finally, add potatoes (cut up) and seasoning. This dish must be cooked slowly and not allowed to get too dry.

Serve very hot with pieces of bread.

Glynn Woodin
Mustard Catering

Babotie

(serves 2)

3/4 lb raw minced mutton	1 medium onion, chopped
1–1 1/2 slices white bread	1–1 1/2 cups milk
2 large eggs	1 tsp curry
1 tsp turmeric	1 tsp sugar
1 tbsp vinegar	4 almonds, blanched and chopped
1 dsrtsp sultanas	1 tbsp chopped dried peach
1 tbsp chopped parsley	3 or 4 bay leaves
1 tbsp butter or oil	salt and pepper

Soak the bread in the milk for about half an hour, then squeeze out.
Fry onion, meat and curry – add turmeric, sugar, vinegar and soaked bread. Add peach, sultanas, almonds and parsley – season and pack into greased oven-proof dish. Beat eggs into squeezed-out milk and pour over the top – place bay leaves on top and dot with butter. Stand dish in a pan of water and bake at 350°F for 1–1 1/2 hours.

Serve with rice and a good fruit chutney.

Sam Torrance

Vegetable Casserole

Ingredients:
carrots
turnip
potato
onion
1/2 pt vegetable stock
Red Leicester cheese

Method:
Slice up all the vegetables and place them layer by layer in a casserole dish, starting with a layer of carrot then a layer of turnip, a layer of onion and a layer of potato. Repeat this layering process until the pot is full, ensuring the final layer is potato.

Lynsey Ann Forbes

Add the vegetable stock and place in a moderate oven for about 1 hour. Once cooked remove from oven and cover the top with a generous helping of grated cheese. Place under the grill until browned.

Ronnie Barker

The £5 note sandwich

Ingredients:-

2 slices wholemeal bread.

Butter (or - low fat substitute)

Gentlemans Relish

One £5 note (fresh, if possible)

½ glass dry white wine

Method:- Prepare the sliced wholemeal bread by spreading with butter (or low-fat substitute) Cut into triangular halves. Drink the ½ glass wine. Place sliced bread together to form sandwich.

Eat with relish, and send £5 note to Cancer Research.

Rose Gray and Ruth Rogers
The River Café
Thames Wharf, London

Salt Cod with Chickpeas
(for 6)

600 g (1 lb 6 oz) salt cod (see below), cut into 5 cm (2 in) pieces
175 g (6 oz) dried chickpeas, soaked overnight
1 large potato, peeled
5 large garlic cloves, peeled and 3 sliced finely
1 sprig each of fresh thyme, bay and sage
3 tablespoons olive oil
2 small dried red chillies, crumbled
1 x 800 g (1 3/4 lb) peeled plum tomatoes, drained of their juices
Maldon salt and freshly ground black pepper
900 g (2 lb) Swiss chard, large stems removed, blanched and roughly chopped
250 ml (8 fl oz) white wine
3 tablespoons chopped fresh flat-leaf parsley

Put the chickpeas into a saucepan with the potato, 2 whole garlic cloves and the herbs. Cover with cold water, bring to the boil and skim the surface. Turn the heat down and simmer for 1–1 1/2 hours. Keep the chickpeas in their cooking liquid until you use them.

Heat 2 tablespoons of oil in a thick-bottomed pan. Add half the sliced garlic, cook to soften a little, then add half the chilli and the tomatoes. Cook for 30 minutes. Season.

Heat the remaining oil in a thick-bottomed pan. Add the rest of the garlic and fry briefly. Place the cod on the garlic, brown on both sides then add the wine. Reduce the heat and simmer for a few minutes until the cod is cooked. Season with pepper and chilli. Add the skinned chickpeas to the tomato sauce. Gently heat for 2–3 minutes then add the chard and the cod, with the pan juices. Sprinkle with the parsley.

Salt cod

It is best to buy a whole cod – of about 2.25–2.75 kg (5–6 lb), say – and to take it home and fillet it yourself. It is important that the salting process is started the moment you have finished filleting in order to prevent deterioration of the cut side of the fish. Maldon salt is not suitable for this recipe.

1 kg (2 1/4 lb) very fresh fillet of cod with skin intact
1 kg (2 1/4 lb) natural coarse sea salt

Use a flat board, and arrange this in a tray, with a saucer placed under one end to make it slant at an angle. Cover the board with a layer of salt about 1 cm (1/2 in) deep. Place the fish, skin side down, on top of the salt. Cover the other side of the fish with 1 cm of salt. Put in the fridge for 24 hours minimum – 5 days maximum.
Remove the salt by rinsing the fish under a running cold tap for 5 minutes. Then place in a bath of water for 6 hours, changing the water as frequently as possible.

© River Café Cook Book Two

The Rt. Hon. Lord Steel of Aikwood

Favourite Recipe for Welsh Rarebit

1/2 lb fresh Cheddar or Cheshire cheese
a little paprika
salt

1/2 tsp dry mustard
a little beer or stout
a few grains cayenne pepper

Miles East

Shred the cheese and put it in a double boiler. Let it melt slowly over hot water kept just under boiling-point. Add mustard, paprika, cayenne and salt to taste according to the needs of the cheese. Then stir in gradually as much beer as the cheese will absorb. The mixture should be smooth and velvety.

Serve on hot buttered toast or hot toasted biscuits.

The Rt. Rev. Lord Sheppard of Liverpool

Pineapple Tuna

(serves 18)

6 tins of tuna in vegetable oil
6 tins of pineapple cubes/pieces
6 medium onions, roughly chopped
2 pints of milk
6 heaped dessertspoons of plain flour
6 heaped dessertspoons of granulated sugar
6 teaspoons of cumin
garam masala and coriander or 6 dessertspoons of
    mild curry powder
12 oz margarine

Christopher Cassell

Fry the onions in margarine. When brown add the flour and blend in. Add the milk, curry/spices and the sugar. Dilute with pineapple juice. Add the tuna, broken up, and pineapple pieces. Serve with rice.

Note: for 4 people use 1 x 7 oz tin tuna, 1 x 15 oz tin pineapple pieces, 1 chopped onion, 1/3 pint milk, 1 heaped dessertspoon each of plain flour and sugar, 1 teaspoon curry/spices and 2 oz margarine.

Delia Smith

Roast Leg of Lamb with Shrewsbury Sauce

(serves 6)

This is my favourite way of cooking lamb at present – plainly roasted with lots of basting to keep it juicy and succulent, then incorporating all the meat juices and crusty bits into what is truly one of the best sauces ever created. It's sweet and sharp at the same time and complements the lamb perfectly.

5 lb (2.25kg) leg of lamb
1 small onion, peeled and sliced

For the Shrewsbury sauce:

1 level tbsp plain flour
1 pint (570ml) beaujolais
3 tbsp Worcestershire sauce
salt and freshly milled black pepper

1 heaped tsp mustard powder
5 rounded tbsp Tiptree redcurrant jelly
juice of 1 lemon

Preheat the oven to gas mark 5, 370°F, 190°C.

First of all place the meat in a good solid roasting tin, tucking the slices of onion in beneath it. Season the surface with salt and freshly milled black pepper, then place it, uncovered, in the preheated oven on the middle shelf. Roast for 30 minutes per pound (for a 5lb /2.25kg leg this will be 2 1/2 hours). Make sure that you baste the lamb at least three times whilst it is cooking, as this will help to keep it juicy and succulent. If you like to serve your lamb quite pink, give it 30 minutes less cooking time and adjust this on the timetable.

To tell if the lamb is cooked to your liking, insert a skewer into the centre, then press; as the juice runs out, you will see to what degree it is cooked – the pinker the juice, the rarer the meat. When it is cooked, remove it to a carving board and keep it in a warm place to rest for 30 minutes.

Now to make the sauce. Spoon off any surplus fat from the tin, tipping it to one side and allowing the fat to separate from the juices. You need to leave about 2 tablespoons of fat behind. Now place the tin over direct heat turned to low. Stir in the flour and mustard powder until you have a smooth paste that has soaked up all the fat and the juices.

Next add the wine, a little at a time, mixing with a wooden spoon after each addition. Halfway through switch from the spoon to a whisk and continue to whisk until all the wine has been incorporated. Now simply add the redcurrant jelly, Worcestershire sauce, lemon juice and seasoning, then whisk again until the jelly has dissolved.

Now turn the heat to its lowest setting and let the sauce gently bubble and reduce slightly for about 15 minutes. Then pour it into a warm serving jug. Carve the lamb, pour over a little of the sauce and hand the rest round separately.

Claire Rayner

This is a main course recipe which comes from the series Kitchen Garden *which was televised some time ago.*

Vegetable Curry
(ample for 6)

Ingredients:
250 ml (1/2 pt) vegetable stock
250 ml (1/2 pt) plain yoghurt
1 chopped cooking apple
12g (1/2 oz) chopped root ginger
clove of garlic chopped
tabasco and Worcester sauces
100–125g (4-5 oz) currants and sultanas
chopped mixed vegetables,
    including skinned tomatoes and onion
50–100g (2–4 oz) chopped nuts
    (peanuts, hazels, cashews, almonds)
1 jar chutney
juice and rind of 1 lemon
curry powder to taste

Catriona Hartley

You need a collection of mixed vegetables – onions, carrots, parsnips, broad beans, potatoes, sliced runner beans, turnip, shredded cabbage and chopped skinned tomatoes. You'll also need a jar of chutney (I use homemade but you can use the bought kind!). Seasoning is curry powder – and you have to use whatever sort suits you best. Real experts mix their own from separate spices, but your local Indian grocery will be glad to advise you.

Now, into a large shallow pan – I use a wok which I bought at a Chinese shop very cheaply, but you can use a large frying pan – fry the onion first in a little oil. Then add the vegetables including the tomatoes and then a little stock, just enough really to moisten it.

Now the chopped apple, the dried fruit, the nuts, the ginger, the lemon juice and rind and the curry powder. Stir it all up together and then add the jar of chutney. That's a lovely shortcut to flavour for curry! Then the tasting starts. Add tabasco and Worcester sauce and garlic and salt and pepper until it tastes right. I can't tell you how much – everyone has their own views on this! Last of all, stir in the yogurt. Now, transfer the whole lot to an oven-to-table dish, and put it in the oven – medium heat (Regulo 4, 375°F, 190°C) – for about an hour. By then all the vegetables will be cooked through and will have taken on the flavour of the curry sauce. By the way, if in the cooking the liquid seems too much – sometimes vegetables throw up a lot of natural juice – add a spoonful or two of bran. Thickens deliciously and easily and very healthily!

Sir Simon Rattle

Salmon by Simon
(or Simplest and Best Salmon)

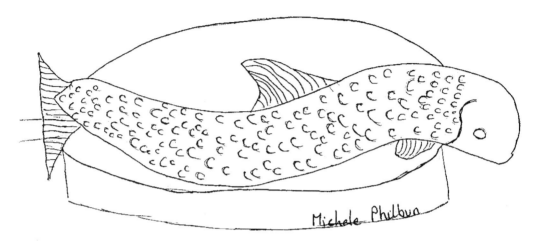

Michele Philbun

Ask the fishmonger to leave the skin on the bottom of tail end salmon fillets. Place, uncovered, in a non stick pan with no oil, for 10 minutes. Then season with plenty of salt and pepper. Cover the pan and cook for 5 minutes maximum.

The fish should turn out crusty, almost caramelised on the bottom and buttery rare in the middle. I eat it with French beans or mangetout – it's so delicious and rich it needs nothing else.

Richard Shepherd
Langan's Brasserie
Stratton Street, London

Carré d'Agneau Rôti aux Herbes de Provence
(serves 4)

2 best ends of lamb, chined and trimmed for roasting
1 bunch of rosemary   salt and pepper
Dijon mustard   oil for roasting

For the persillage:
100 gm butter   50 gm shallots, chopped and cooked in white wine
50 gm parsley, chopped   225 gm fine white breadcrumbs

Preheat the oven to gas mark 7 (220°C/425°F).

Richard Shepherd's *Carré d'Agneau Rôti continued*

Prepare persillage by melting butter and adding other ingredients. Mix well. Persillage should be soft, not sloppy.

Heat roasting tray in the oven. Season the racks of lamb with salt, pepper and rosemary. Add a little oil to the roasting tray, place lamb in tray fat side down and cook for 4–5 minutes.

Turn lamb on to bones and cook for a further 4–5 minutes, or until pink. (*Note:* if it is not new season lamb, longer cooking times are required.)

Remove lamb from tray and leave to rest for 5 minutes in a warm place.

Brush back of lamb with Dijon mustard. Spread the persillage as thinly as possible over the lamb, pressing firmly to make it stick.

Glaze under a hot grill until persillage is evenly browned, then cut into cutlets and serve with gravy made from pan juices deglazed with a little stock.

Sir Harry Secombe

Myra's Stuffed Aubergines
(serves 8)

2 lb lean minced beef
8 oz chopped onions
clove of garlic
mixed herbs
1/2 pt tomato juice
dash of Worcester sauce
3 tsp Bovril
black pepper
8 aubergines
breadcrumbs

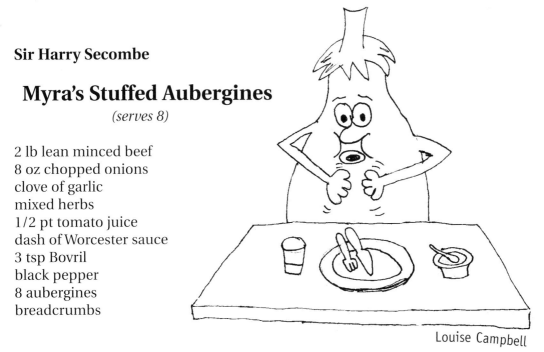

Louise Campbell

Put minced beef in a heavy-based saucepan, cover with water and bring to the boil for 5 minutes. Pour off liquid, then add onions, crushed garlic, herbs and tomato juice. Mix Bovril and Worcester sauce with a little hot water and add to the mince. Simmer for 45 minutes or until tender.

Place aubergines in water and simmer until the skins start to wrinkle (do not over cook). Cut in half and scoop out flesh and mix with the minced beef. Fill the aubergine shells with the mixture and bake in a moderate oven for 30 minutes. Cover with fine breadcrumbs and place under the grill to brown.

Serve at once.

Andrew Radford
Atrium
Cambridge Street, Edinburgh

Roast Halibut with Parmesan and Leek Crumb and Autumn Chanterelle

(serves 4)

Ingredients:

4 x 4–6 oz halibut portions (or cod, hake or common sole)
2 oz brioche crumbs
12 oz mushrooms, (eg chanterelle, hedge-hog, field)
olive oil

8 oz leek, finely diced
2 oz parmesan, grated
salt and pepper
parsley, chopped

Method:

Place the 4 halibut portions on an oiled baking tray, brush with olive oil and season. Cook under a grill or roast in a hot oven for 3 or 4 minutes.

Mix the parmesan, leek and brioche crumbs and sprinkle on to the halibut. Place under the grill to brown.

Meanwhile pan fry the chopped shallots and mushrooms in hot oil for approximately a minute.

Place a little of the mushroom mixture on to each plate and on top of this place a piece of halibut. Drizzle with a little quality olive oil, sprinkle with parsley and serve.

Roast Venison, Garlic and Mixed Mushrooms

(serves 4)

One of the great autumn/winter dishes. Venison can be replaced by beef or lamb in the spring or duck in autumn.

Ingredients:

4 x 4–6 oz portions venison loin
8/10 oz mixed mushrooms
1 oz shallots, finely diced
1/2 pt brown stock
parsley

For the garlic confit:
12/16 cloves garlic
sunflower or virgin olive oil
4 bay leaves or 4 thyme sprigs or 2–3 of both

Method:

Pour the brown stock into a saucepan, add the garlic trimmings and put on the heat to reduce. Later strain before serving.

For the garlic confit: Half fill a small saucepan with olive oil/sunflower oil and heat to about 60°. Add the thyme/bay leaves and garlic, and place in an oven, gas mark 1, until the garlic is cooked (20/30 minutes). Strain. Discard the thyme/bay and retain the garlic oil for cooking or to add to a salad dressing.

Pan fry the venison for 1–2 minutes on each side, then place in a high oven for 4–5 minutes. Remove, cover and leave to rest.

Andrew Radford's *Roast Venison continued*

For the assembly: Fry the shallots, add the mushrooms and the garlic confit and cook for 1–2 minutes. Divide this between 4 plates. Carve the venison pieces into two. Place two halves on top of the garlic/mushroom mix per plate. Pour a little of the stock over, sprinkle with parsley and serve.

Katie Stewart

Chicken with New Potatoes in Roquefort Cream Sauce
(serves 4)

Ingredients:

4 chicken thighs
450g (1 lb) new potatoes
75 ml (3 fl oz) dry white wine
150 ml (1/4 pt) chicken stock
1 level tsp herbes de Provence
freshly milled pepper

4 chicken drumsticks
25g (1 oz) butter
2 cloves garlic
3 tbsp double cream
100 g (4 oz) roquefort cheese

Method:

Trim the chicken pieces and scrub the new potatoes. Melt the butter in a large frying pan, add the chicken pieces and fry to brown them on all sides. Remove the chicken from the pan. Add the potatoes to the hot butter, turn to coat them all over, then sauté for just a few minutes until they are beginning to take colour. With a slotted spoon, transfer the potatoes to a flame-proof casserole and place the chicken pieces on top. Peel and crush the garlic.

Add the white wine to the hot pan drippings and stir to pick up all the flavouring bits. Add the chicken stock, the crushed garlic and the herbes de Provence. Bring to the boil, then pour the contents of the pan over the chicken and new potatoes.

Cover with the casserole lid and simmer gently for 20–25 minutes or until the chicken is tender and the potatoes cooked.

Add the double cream and crumbled roquefort cheese and stir until the cheese has melted. Season with freshly milled pepper and serve.

Caroline Waldegrave
(Principal, Leith's School of Food and Wine)

I enclose a recipe for Salmon Olives with Herb Sauce which I cooked a few times this summer for my friends and family. It is straight forward to make, very delicious as well as being healthy. It comes from Leith's Easy Dinner Parties *written by Caroline Waldegrave, Puff Fairclough and Janey Orr.*

Salmon Olives with Herb Sauce
(serves 6)

3 x 270g/10oz salmon tail fillets, skinned
oil
juice of 1 lemon
3 tbsp dry white wine
salt and freshly ground black pepper
1 bay leaf
3 cloves of garlic, unpeeled
55g/2oz dry white breadcrumbs
finely grated zest of 3 limes
3 tablespoons finely chopped dill

For the herb sauce:
6 tbsp good quality olive oil
2 tbsp white wine vinegar
2 tbsp finely chopped dill
2 tbsp finely chopped parsley
1 tsp Dijon mustard

For the garnish:
sprigs of dill
lime wedges

Method:
Preheat the oven to 200C/400F/gas mark 6.
Trim the salmon fillets and remove any bones. Slice each salmon fillet in half horizontally. Put each slice between 2 pieces of clingfilm and beat them out carefully with a rolling pin or heavy saucepan to increase the size by about a quarter.
Place the cloves of garlic on a baking sheet, brush with a little oil and bake in the oven for about 10 minutes until soft. Peel and crush the garlic and mix with the breadcrumbs, lime zest and dill. Season to taste with salt and pepper. Divide the mixture between the 6 slices of salmon and roll them up towards the narrow end.
Put the salmon olives on to a large sheet of lightly oiled kitchen foil and brush with oil. Sprinkle with the lemon juice and white wine and season lightly. Add the bay leaf and fold up the edges of the foil to form a loosely wrapped but securely sealed parcel. Put on to a baking sheet and bake in the oven for 10 minutes.

Meanwhile, make the herb sauce: combine all the ingredients in a liquidiser or food processor and process until smooth.
When the salmon olives are cooked, add 2 tablespoons of the hot cooking liquid from the parcel to the sauce and process again briefly.
Season to taste with salt and pepper.
Lift the salmon olives from the foil, drain and cut each olive in half on the diagonal.

To serve: flood 6 plates with the herb sauce and put 2 pieces of salmon on each plate. Garnish each with a sprig of dill and a lime wedge.

A recommended wine to accompany this dish is New Zealand Sauvignon Blanc.

House of Lords

Mrs Belinda Pinckney
Cancer Research Campaign
The Garden House
Balthayock
Perth PH2 7LG

27 August 1997

Dear Mrs. Pinkney,

I am delighted to send very best wishes for your efforts to raise funds through your Celebrity Cook Book for the Cancer Research Campaign in Scotland.

I know how very important Cancer Research is and I am therefore delighted to commend your book, which I know will raise substantial funds for further research.

My own personal receipe for life is a strong faith and a wish to succeed and achieve. I've had a good life and your efforts, I know, will enable others to be helped .

Yours very sincerely

George Tonypandy

John Webber
Kinnaird, Perthshire

Honey Roast Breast of Quail
served on a crisp potato cake with an essence of wild mushrooms
(serves 4)

Rachel Robertson

10 oven-ready whole quail
heather honey
French mustard
8 oz leaf spinach (picked and washed)
1 garlic clove
lardons of smoked bacon
4 large potatoes
6 dried morels (soaked overnight)

4 oz assorted, fresh wild mushrooms
1 1/4 pt beef stock
5 fl oz red wine
3 fl oz Madeira
4 oz mixed vegetables (carrot, onion,
　celery), peeled and chopped
arrowroot

Singe the quail over a gas flame or blow lamp to remove remaining feathers. Cut off the winglets at the first joint, clean the wing bone and take out the wish bone.

Remove the legs by cutting diagonally downwards behind the breasts. Set the breasts aside for a moment, then roughly chop the legs two or three times to break them down.

Take a stainless thick-bottomed pan and heat well, add a drop of oil and throw in the quail legs, tossing them over in the pan until evenly coloured. Add the chopped vegetables, reduce the heat slightly, cook for 3–4 minutes, then drain off as much fat as possible from the pan. Return the contents to the pan and add the beef stock. Bring the pan up to a slow simmer, skim off any scum that has formed and cook steadily for 40 minutes.

Grate a potato and press out the water. Season lightly then using a small frying pan cook the potato in a little oil, pressing it down well to form a cake about 1 cm thick. Cook on both sides to a golden brown and keep warm. You will require 4 in all.

Strain off the stock and pass through a muslin cloth. Take a clean pan and in it bring the red wine, Madeira and morel water to the boil. Reduce the liquid by half, then add the infused stock. Reduce the volume by about half again and then add the fresh mushrooms and morels.

Bring the sauce gently back to the simmer and allow to reduce slowly until the flavour is right. Lightly thicken with arrowroot. Cover and set aside. While the sauce is reducing, season the quail breasts and cook gently in a mixture of oil and butter on top of the stove. Don't be tempted to cook them in the oven as this will dry out the meat.

When the quail breasts are just cooked but still pink, remove them from the pan and place them on to a warm plate to relax.

In a clean pan melt butter with the garlic clove and bacon. Add the washed spinach leaves. Cook over a medium heat keeping the spinach moving around the pan. The spinach should be cooked in 3–4 minutes. Do not allow to become over-cooked.

Remove the breasts of quail from the carcass and place on a heat-proof plate. Brush with the mustard, then honey and glaze them under a very hot grill or by using a blow-torch.

Take four hot 12" plates, or the largest you have, and place a potato cake in the centre of each. Pile some of the hot spinach on to each potato cake, then arrange five of the quail breasts, point uppermost, on the spinach. The result should look a bit like an Indian wigwam.

Spoon the hot sauce around the potato, arranging the mushrooms as you go, and decorate with picked chervil or parsley.

Fillet of Turbot with a Potato and Parsley Crust

(serves 4)

4 x 5 oz fillets of turbot (free of skin and bone)

12 oz peeled potatoes	2 egg yolks
plain flour	1/2 oz chopped parsley
6 oz leek cut in 1 cm squares	10 fl oz white wine fish sauce
4 oz peeled tomato flesh in 5 mm squares	a few chives

Cut the potatoes into thin strips no more than 3mm squares using a mandolin cutter if you have one. Wash the potatoes to remove the starch and dry the strips well on a towel. Fry the potatoes in a deep fat fryer at 150°C for 2 minutes so that they are three-quarters cooked without colour. Drain well and very carefully fold in a pinch of flour, the parsley, egg yolks and seasoning.

Lightly season the fish and dust in flour. Spread a layer of the potato mixture about 3mm thick on top of the fish, slightly overlapping the potato on the edges. Place the fish in the fridge until needed.

Plunge the leek into boiling salted water for 3 minutes, then refresh in ice-cold water. Drain and set aside.

To serve, sauté the fish in a little hot oil, placing the potato side down first. Cook on a good heat to colour the potato, then reduce the heat and add a knob of butter to the pan. Allow to cook for about 4 minutes in all, then carefully turn the fish over and cook for a further minute.

Warm the leeks in a little butter, lightly seasoning, and warm the tomato under the grill. Bring the sauce to the simmer and add the chives. Arrange the leeks in the centre of the plate, allowing some to be seen around the fish. Place the hot fish on the leeks and scatter the tomato around. Pour a thin border of sauce around the fish and serve at once.

Mandy Wagstaff

Thai Red Chicken Curry

(serves 4)

This recipe is perfect for a last-minute supper. Once the curry paste has been prepared, the finishing off takes just a few minutes. I make a larger batch of the curry paste and store it in the refrigerator for up to two weeks.

If kaffir lime leaves are not available use the zest of one lime instead. Most of the other ingredients are available from the larger supermarkets or from Thai food stores.

For the curry paste:
1 tsp coriander seeds
6 black peppercorns
4 garlic cloves, peeled
1 stalk lemon grass, finely shredded

6 red chillis, roughly chopped
1 tsp cumin seeds
1/2 tsp coarse sea salt
2 Kaffir lime leaves, shredded
1 inch piece of root ginger, grated

4 chicken breasts, skinned
200 ml canned coconut milk
100 ml chicken stock
1 tsp brown sugar
2 tbsp fish sauce (Nam Pla)

Thai basil leaves

Begin by making the curry paste: in a dry frying pan lightly cook the coriander and cumin seeds for 1–2 minutes to release the flavours. Transfer to a pestle and mortar with the peppercorns and sea salt and grind to a powder. Add the garlic cloves along with the lime leaves and lemon grass. Pound to release the juices then add the ginger and chillis. Continue pounding to a smooth paste. Of course, this can be done in the small bowl of a food processor but somehow there is a great deal of satisfaction in preparing the paste by hand.

Cut the chicken into large pieces and mix into the curry paste. If time permits leave to marinate for half an hour. Heat a large heavy-based frying pan over a medium heat and cook the chicken pieces for 2 minutes, stir in the coconut milk with the chicken stock. Add the sugar and the fish sauce and simmer gently for 5–6 minutes or until the chicken is thoroughly cooked. Adjust the seasoning.

Tear up the basil leaves and sprinkle over. Serve with steamed fragrant rice.

Victoria Wood

Children's Vegetable Stew

Chop an onion and soften it in butter or oil. Get all the old root veg out from the fridge. Wash it (I skip this stage if I'm really busy, figuring the cooking will loosen the dirt). Chop it down to mouth size and bung it in with the onion.

Pour on as much hot water as is in the kettle. Put in a bit of Vecon (veg stock) or Marmite and some herbs. If your children don't like herbs, tell them it's grass. Add the pot barley which you should have soaked overnight but I forgot to mention it. Go and do the washing. When you smell burning the barley's caught and it should be cooked. Slop it on the plates anyhow and ignore any howling.

Philip Powell

Terry Wogan
(This recipe was very kindly sent by his wife, Helen, on his behalf.)

Twice Cooked Fillet of Beef

3 lb fillet beef	1 tsp herbes de Provence
3 level tbsp Dijon mustard	2 tsp grated ginger
1 tbsp soya sauce	1 tbsp olive oil
1 clove garlic	salt and pepper

Method:
Mix all the above ingredients, apart from the beef, together in a bowl and beat in the olive oil.
Coat the meat all over with the marinade using a pastry brush and leave to rest for two hours at room temperature before cooking the first time.
Pre-heat oven to 200°C and cook for exactly 32 minutes.
Take out of oven and allow to cool.
In the evening cook again at the same temperature for a further 16 minutes.
Serve with the following red wine sauce:

Red wine sauce (simple method):

1 1/2 cups water	2 shallots, chopped
2 beef stock cubes	1 sprig parsley
1 cup dry red wine	1 bay leaf
2 tbsp tomato paste	2 tsp plain flour
60g butter	redcurrant jelly

Combine water, crumbled stock cubes, wine, tomato paste, shallots, parsley and bay leaf in small saucepan. Bring to the boil, reduce heat and simmer until reduced by half. Strain and discard shallot mixture.
Pour any pan drippings from beef into small saucepan, add flour and cook, stirring, until brown. Gradually add wine mixture. Bring to boil stirring constantly. Reduce heat and simmer uncovered for a few minutes.
Gradually whisk in small pieces of cold butter over heat, whisking well after each addition.
I also add about a dessertspoon of redcurrant jelly which gives it a good flavour.

Auberon Waugh

Bacon and Marmite Sandwich

One of the best and simplest lunches is the Bacon and Marmite Sandwich. This should be made with granary bread, well spread with butter and a thin coating of Marmite. The bacon should be without its rind and grilled until it is crisp and dry. It is the sort of lunch which needs no alcoholic accompaniment and will keep any working man happy until dinner time.

Ian Woosnam

After a hard day on the golf course, I love to come home to my favourite meal of

Woosie's Shepherd's Pie

Preparation time: 20 minutes
Cooking time: 30 minutes

Ingredients: (for 4-6)

2 finely chopped onions	4–6 diced carrots
3 oz unsalted butter	1 lb cooked minced beef
6 fl oz beef stock or gravy	1 level tbsp tomato ketchup
1/4 tsp Worcestershire sauce	salt and black pepper
2–3 tbsp milk	1 lb mashed potatoes

Method:

Cook the onions in 1 oz of the butter until soft, add the meat and carrots and cook until lightly brown. Stir in the stock, ketchup and Worcestershire sauce. Season.

Beat the remaining melted butter and the milk into the potatoes. Put the meat in a greased ovenproof dish, cover with potato and ripple the top with a fork.

Bake near the top of an oven heated to 420°F or Gas Mark 7 for 30 minutes or until brown.

Serve the pie hot, on its own or with green vegetables.

Ailie Davidson

Woosie's Shepherd's Pie

Mike Picken
Executive Chef
Gleneagles Hotel
Perthshire

Haggis
with Deep Fried Vegetables,
Herb Crumble and Dalwhinnie Sauce
(serves 4)

4 savoury short crust tartlets 2" diameter
12 oz haggis
4 oz brioche bread
2 oz parsley / coriander / chervil
1 carrot / beetroot / leek
6 oz cooked mashed swede
6 oz cooked mashed potato
6 fl oz beef gravy
2 tbsp cream
2 fl oz Dalwhinnie whisky

Tartlet:
Heat the haggis with a little stock and fill the tartlets to full.
Place the brioche bread cut into rough cubes into a blender with the herbs and blend for approximately 2 minutes.
This should make a green herb crumble. Sprinkle this on top of the tartlet and lightly brown under the grill.

Deep fried vegetables:
Slice the carrot and beetroot very thinly and cut the leeks to give 2" sheets.
Individually deep fry these in hot oil until crispy and lightly coloured. Drain on paper. This should be done beforehand.

Clapshott:
Mix the hot puréed swede together with the potato to give a marble effect. This is known as clapshott.

Sauce:
Heat the beef gravy with the Dalwhinnie whisky and add the cream.

To present:
Place a spoonful of the clapshott on the plate with the tartlet and vegetables resting on it. Pour the whisky sauce among the four plates equally, and serve.

Lorna Wing

Rustic Sage and Onion Chicken Stew
with Rigatoni

(serves 10)

2 fl oz olive oil
2 large onions, chopped
2 large carrots, peeled and sliced
1 lb tinned chopped plum tomatoes
1/2 oz capers
2 tbsp sage, chopped

2 lb boned chicken pieces
6 oz rindless streaky bacon or pancetta, chopped
1/2 pint red wine vinegar
1 oz anchovy fillets, chopped
1 pint red wine
ground black pepper

1 lb rigatoni
2 oz butter
1 oz parmesan
ground black pepper

Heat the oil in a sauté pan and fry the chicken on both sides until well browned. Remove from the pan and transfer to a casserole.

Add the onion and bacon or pancetta to the pan and fry in the residual oil until the onions are soft and the bacon is crisp. Stir in the carrots and cook for 3–4 minutes.

Add the tomatoes, anchovies, capers, red wine, red wine vinegar and sage. Season with black pepper. Bring to the boil and then pour over the chicken. Cover and cook in a pre-heated oven at 375°F/190°C/gas mark 5 for 45 minutes or until the chicken is cooked.

Cook the rigatoni in boiling salted water for 10–12 minutes or until *al dente*. Drain and add the butter, parmesan and black pepper. Serve hot with the chicken.

Fatima Whitbread

Fish Pie

(serves 4)

Fish Pie
(Serves 4)

Wayne Cochrane

1 lb (450g) haddock fillet
bay leaf
1 onion
2 hard-boiled eggs
1 beaten egg for glazing
2 lb (900g) potatoes
2 1/2 oz (65g) butter

1/2 pt (300ml) milk and an extra 6 tbsp
6 peppercorns
3 level tbsp flour
5 fl oz (150ml) fresh single cream
4 oz (125g) cooked prawns
2 tbsp chopped fresh parsley

Clean and dry the fish.

In a saucepan, place fish, 1/2 pint (300ml) of milk, the bay leaf, peppercorns and chopped onion; bring to boil and simmer for 10 minutes.

Peel and boil the potatoes, then mash. Heat the 6 tbsp (90ml) of milk with 1oz (25g) of butter and beat into the mashed potatoes – season to taste.

Lift the fish out of the liquid, remove the skin and any bones; strain the liquid into a jug and save for later.

Melt 1 1/2oz (40g) butter in a saucepan, stir in the flour and cook gently for 1 minute, stirring all the time. Take off the heat and gradually stir in the saved liquid. Bring to the boil, stirring all the time, until the sauce thickens. Cook for a further 2–3 minutes.

Roughly chop the hard-boiled eggs and add to the sauce along with the cream, fish, parsley and prawns.

Season to taste and place the mixture into a 2-pint (1.1 litre) pie dish.

Spoon the mashed potatoes into a piping bag and pipe across the fish mixture.

Bake at gas mark 6 (200°C/400°F) for 10–15 minutes until the potato sets. Brush the beaten egg over the pie and return it to the oven for a further 15 minutes or until golden brown.

Sir Cliff Richard

Chicken "à la Pope"

(serves 6)

Ingredients:
1x3 1/2 lb chicken
2 pkts frozen broccoli
4 tbs mayonnaise
2 cans Campbell's condensed
Cream of Chicken Soup
1 soup can full of milk
half tsp curry powder
3 oz Cheddar cheese, grated
2 pkts crisps or
4 slices bread, crumbled
1 oz white wine
1 tsp lemon juice
margarine

Method:
Cook chicken until tender.
Cool. Strip off meat and cut into pieces.
Cook broccoli until tender, and drain.
Grease ovenproof baking dish.
Place chicken on bottom with broccoli on top.
Mix the mayonnaise, soup, milk, curry powder,
lemon juice and wine.
Cook on low for 20 minutes (150°C).
Sprinkle breadcrumbs or crisps and cheese
over the top and dot with margarine.
Bake at 180°C until brown on top
(approx. 20 minutes).

Richard Branson

Bobotie

(serves 3–4)

1 tablespoon oil
1 large onion, finely chopped
450g / 1 lb lean mince
50g / 2 oz flaked almonds
1 apple, peeled and chopped
1 tablespoon curry powder
1 tablespoon mango chutney
40g / 1 1/2 oz sultanas
1 tablespoon lemon juice
150 ml / 1/4 pint beef stock or red wine

Topping:
2 free range eggs
20g / 3/4 oz flour
20g / 3/4 oz butter
300 ml / 1/2 pint milk
salt and pepper

Set oven at 180°C / 350°F / Gas Mark 4.
Fry onion until transparent.
Add the minced meat and brown.
Add the chopped apple, curry powder, almonds and sultanas.
Cook for about 5 minutes, then add chutney, stock/wine and lemon juice.
Add salt and pepper to taste and possibly a little more curry powder.
Then transfer to a pie dish and bake in the oven for 15 minutes.
Meanwhile, make the topping.
Melt butter, add flour and stir in milk, being careful not to let the sauce go lumpy.
When the sauce has thickened take off heat and allow to cool slightly before adding eggs.
Stir them in and add salt and pepper.
Remove main dish from oven (it should have formed a slight crust) and pour the sauce over it.
Return to the oven and bake for about 40 minutes until the top is slightly browned.
Serve with rice and salad.

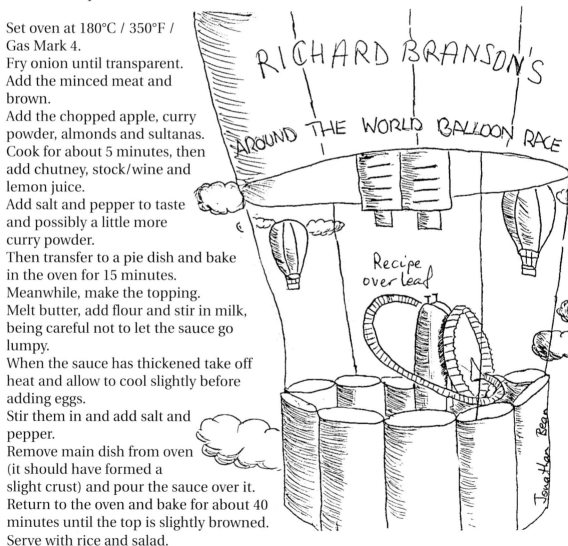

RICHARD BRANSON'S
AROUND THE WORLD BALLOON RACE

Recipe over leaf

Jonathan Bean

David and Hilary Brown
La Potiniere
Gullane, Scotland

Chicken Breast with Onion Confit and Mustard Sauce

(6 servings)

6 fresh, skinned chicken breasts, weighing 4–5 oz (100–150g) each,
trimmed of any small pieces of bone and fat
seasoning
1/2 oz (15g) unsalted butter

Mustard sauce:
5 fl oz (150ml) Chambrey vermouth
5 fl oz (150ml) chicken stock
7 1/2 fl oz (225ml) double cream
2 teaspoons moutarde de Meaux
seasoning

To serve and garnish:
6 generous tablespoons onion confit *(see page 126)*
fresh parsley

Preheat oven to 475°F (240°C) Gas 9, or as high as possible.

For the sauce, place the wine in a small pan, bring to the boil, then simmer until reduced to 2 tablespoons. Add the stock, bring back to the boil, then simmer until reduced by half. Add the cream and simmer until a light coating consistency is achieved. Set aside.

Meanwhile, lightly season the chicken breasts on the cut side with salt. Place them, salted side down, on a lightly buttered baking tray. Melt the 1/2 oz (15g) butter and use this to brush over the breasts. Season with a little more salt.

Bake the chicken breasts on the middle shelf of the preheated oven for 9 minutes.

Gently reheat the onion confit, being careful not to allow it to scorch, stirring frequently with a wooden spoon.

Reheat the sauce, whisk in the mustard, then taste for seasoning. Add a little salt and freshly ground black pepper if necessary.

Remove the breasts from the oven. Place a good tablespoon of the onion confit on each warmed serving plate, slice the chicken in slices 1/4 in (6mm) thick and place these, overlapping, on top of it. Spoon the sauce over or around the chicken and sprinkle with finely chopped parsley. Serve immediately.

Onion Confit

(8 servings)

This is a highly flavoured, well reduced, tasty mixture of sliced onion, sugar, sherry vinegar and Crème de Cassis. It can be used like chutney, or as a bed for meats such as chicken or duck breast. A little goes a long way as it is so intense. Although you need to caramelise the onions, avoid burning as this will produce a bitter taste.

1 1/2 oz (40g) butter
2 lb (900g) onions, peeled and finely sliced
4 oz (100g) demerara sugar
3 tablespoons sherry vinegar
1 1/2 tablespoons Crème de Cassis
2 teaspoons salt

Melt the butter in a medium-sized saucepan and when it starts to turn light brown, add the onions. Stir together and cook gently for 5 minutes, stirring with a wooden spoon now and again.

Add the remaining ingredients, including the salt, stir together, then simmer un-covered for 1 1/2–2 hours. The time required will depend on the size of your pan, the heat and even the onions, as some are more watery than others. Stir occasionally in order to prevent the mixture from sticking and scorching. The finished "marmalade" should look dark golden and sticky.

Use the onion confit as required while still hot or transfer to a bowl and cover when cold. Due to the high sugar content, this will keep for weeks in the refrigerator. Make sure that it is well sealed as its smell may affect other foods in the refrigerator. Make a larger quantity if you want to have some on hand in the future, to add interest to meat, fish or cheese dishes.

Elizabeth Hurley

Shepherd's Pie

(serves 6)

This is my all-time favourite recipe which was taught to me by my father, although he uses beef instead of lamb, which of course you could do too. I don't really measure or weigh anything when I make this so feel free to use more or less of most things, i.e. carrots, onions, etc. This is even better if you make the meat part a day early and refrigerate it overnight. Mash the potato the next day, slap it on top of the cold meat and bake it in the oven for about 45 minutes. I usually serve it with a large green salad.

2 lb ground lamb	1 large onion, chopped	fresh rosemary
4 large carrots	olive oil	salt and pepper
tomato paste	1 pint stock	red wine
4 lb potatoes	butter	milk

Elizabeth Hurley's *Shepherd's Pie continued*

WOOF

BAAA

SHEPHERD'S PIE

Martin Hodge

Heat some olive oil in a large skillet and gently fry the onion until soft. Add the sliced carrots and cook for a further five minutes. Now add the raw lamb, quickly stirring with a wooden spoon so that most of the meat can get seared by the hot fat. After a few minutes pour some red wine over the meat – you choose how much, I normally use a glass or two. This will make everything start sizzling so keep stirring. Throw in some sprigs of rosemary, a squirt of tomato paste, a good pinch of salt and some freshly ground pepper. Make up a pint of stock – lamb, chicken or vegetable – and add about half to the skillet. Stir it in and turn the heat down to low. Keep an eye on this for the next thirty minutes as it cooks, adding more stock when necessary. The ideal consistency should be rich, moist and glossy with no more than a few tablespoons of liquid. Keep tasting as it cooks and add more salt and pepper if you think it's needed.

Meanwhile boil the potatoes in plenty of salted water until they're soft. Drain them thoroughly and then mash them ferociously with a large knob of butter, a good splash of milk and plenty of black pepper.

Transfer the meat when it's ready into an oven-proof dish and spoon the mashed potato on top of it. Make furrows in the top of the potato with a fork. Put the dish at the top of a hot oven for five minutes or so until the top is brown and crispy.

Jane Clarke
Nutrition Dietetic Consultant

Caramelised Artichoke, Goat's Cheese and Tomato Toasts

(serves 2–4)

1 tin of artichoke hearts, cut into
   halves
2 cloves garlic, finely chopped
1 tbsp fine virgin olive oil
4 ripe tomatoes, halved
1 tbsp fresh basil, finely chopped
3 tsp tomato purée
4 wholegrain or granary rolls, halved
4 large slices of goat's cheese
a handful of pitted Kalamata olives
salt and freshly ground black pepper

Drain the artichoke hearts thoroughly.

Mix the olive oil with 2 cloves of finely chopped garlic.
Drizzle a little of this oil on to a non-stick baking tray. Place the halved artichokes onto the oiled tray, sprinkle with half of the chopped basil and season.

Spread the halved tomatoes with tomato purée and the remainder of the basil. Place beside the dressed artichoke hearts and set under a preheated grill.

Cook for a few minutes, until they are about 3/4 done, remove and place the fillings on top of the halved rolls. Place the sliced goat's cheese and olives on top of the filling, before returning to the grill to melt the cheese and lightly brown.

Leave for a few minutes before serving so that the tomatoes have had a chance to cool slightly.

I suggest you serve this with a crisp green salad. Try to include a strong dark lettuce such as Cos, as this matches the strong tomato flavour.

This is a very quick, but delicious supper dish. Tinned artichokes are excellent to have in the cupboard. They grill beautifully and friends think you've spent hours preparing the fresh ones! The colour combinations of the deep red tomatoes and basil make it a very impressive dish to serve as an after theatre supper or for Sunday brunch.

Ernie Wise

Chicken à la King

(serves 2–3)

1 medium-sized chopped green pepper
50g/2oz butter
1/4 tsp olive or corn oil
100g/4oz sliced mushrooms and stalks
25g/1oz flour
150ml/1/4 pt chicken stock or water
150g/1/4 pt milk
400g/12oz cooked chicken, cut into
    bite-size pieces
150ml/1/4 pt fresh single cream
yolks of 2 standard eggs
1 tbsp dry sherry or lemon juice
seasoning to taste

Fry green pepper gently in butter and oil for five
minutes. Add mushrooms and stalks.
Fry gently with pepper for further five minutes.
Remove from pan and transfer to plate.
Stir flour into remaining butter and oil in pan.
Cook for two minutes without browning.
Gradually blend in stock or water and milk.
Cook, stirring, until sauce comes to boil and
thickens. Lower heat.
Add green pepper, mushrooms and chicken.
Cover pan. Heat through gently for ten minutes.
Beat cream with egg yolks and sherry or lemon
juice. Add to chicken mixture.
Cook for further two to three minutes without boiling.
Season to taste with salt and pepper.

Joanna Trollope

This recipe is the invention of another writer, Angela Huth, who is also an excellent cook. I've used it over and over again – it's quick, simple, delicious and it always works, which is all I require of any recipe.

Honey and Ginger Lamb

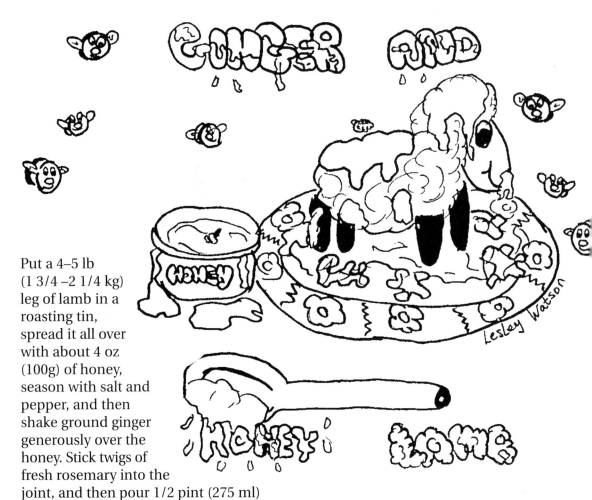

Put a 4–5 lb (1 3/4 –2 1/4 kg) leg of lamb in a roasting tin, spread it all over with about 4 oz (100g) of honey, season with salt and pepper, and then shake ground ginger generously over the honey. Stick twigs of fresh rosemary into the joint, and then pour 1/2 pint (275 ml) of dry cider into the roasting tin. Roast at 400°F, 200°C or gas 6, for 20 minutes per pound, basting frequently, and adding more cider if necessary. You will find that the cider, honey and meat juices have made a most delicious gravy all by themselves, which only needs to have the fat skimmed off it before serving.

Sir Dirk Bogarde

Sussex Stewed Steak

(serves 6)

You will need:

2 1/2 lb sliced best rump steak or chuck
salt and pepper   flour
large onion sliced   3 oz Guinness
3 oz port   2 good tbsp mushroom ketchup

Season meat and smother in flour. Put in shallow ovenproof dish so that it is neat and flat. Place onion slices on top in an even layer. Add stout, port and ketchup. Cover with foil tightly. Place in oven at Mark 1, 275°F for 3 hours. Serve with milk/butter mashed potato and wild mushrooms, *not* button mushrooms, they must be as wild as you can find.

Sir Charles Mackerras

Anchovy Surprise

as invented by Lady Mackerras
(and a great favourite with the whole family in the summer!)

1 lb spinach (either fresh or frozen)
2 hard boiled eggs
2 tins of sardines in olive oil
1 tin anchovy fillets
juice of 1 lemon
tarragon, mayonnaise, salt and
  pepper

Cook and drain the spinach and chop fine.

Put in a mixing bowl and add sardines (drain off some of the oil) and hard boiled eggs (mashed), (keep back a tablespoonful for decoration).

Add lemon juice, tarragon, mayonnaise (2 dessertspoonfuls) and salt and pepper to taste.

Mix all ingredients well together and arrange on a circular plate.

Decorate with hard boiled egg in the centre and anchovies.
Serve *cold.*

Excellent with Orvieto!

131

Evelyn Glennie

Mushroom Crumble
(serves 2)

3 oz wholemeal breadcrumbs
6 oz ground mixed nuts (the chopped
    pack version is crunchier)
4 fl oz oil
1 clove garlic, crushed
1 teaspoon mixed herbs (or fresh
    parsley)

8 oz mushrooms, sliced
1 tablespoon oil
1 large onion, sliced
1 oz flour
1/4 pint stock
salt and pepper to taste

Set oven at 220°C / 425°F / Gas mark 7.

Mix together breadcrumbs, mixed nuts,
garlic and herbs.
Pour over the oil and mix well. Leave on
one side (an hour or more lets the garlic
permeate).

Heat the tablespoon of oil in a frying pan and fry the
onion until soft and brown. Add mushrooms and cook a few minutes more.
Sprinkle in flour and cook for 2 minutes.

Remove from heat and add stock, stirring all the time.
Return to heat and cook until thick. Season.

Pour this mixture into the bottom of an ovenproof casserole and sprinkle the
crumble mixture over it.

Bake in the hot oven for 30 minutes.

Serve with vegetables and salad.

David Wilson
The Peat Inn
Peat Inn
Cupar, Fife

Medallions of Monkfish and Lobster
with Asparagus and Wild Mushroom in a Lobster Sauce
(serves 4)

Ingredients:
450g monkfish, boned and trimmed
1 large lobster, about 680g
225g asparagus
350g wild mushrooms (chanterelle or similar)
100g potato
100g carrot
salt and pepper
oil for frying
butter for frying

For the sauce:
50g each onion and celery
50g each fennel and carrot
1 clove garlic
100g shells/claws lobster
1/4 of a 20 oz tin plum tomatoes
1 level tsp tomato purée
1 level tbsp brandy
3 fl oz white wine
3 peppercorns
bouquet garni**
1/2 pt fish stock
2 oz butter
olive oil for frying

**(tarragon/chervil/flat
parsley/ thyme/ bayleaf)

To make sauce:
1. Sweat vegetables in a little olive oil.
2. Add shells, brandy, and flame off. Add white wine.
3. Add tomatoes, purée, peppercorns, stock and bouquet garni.
4. Bring to boil, simmer for 1–1 1/2 hours.
5. Pass through sieve, then add butter over heat.
6. Check seasoning.

Method:
1. Make sauce in advance and refrigerate until required.
2. Wash and trim asparagus. Cook in boiling, salted water until tender. Refresh in ice-cold water. Reserve.
3. Wash and peel both potato and carrot. Dice (approx. 3/8") and cook until tender. Refresh and reserve.
4. Clean and pick over the mushrooms.
5. Remove lobster from shell.
6. Put a little oil in a sauté pan. When hot, add mushrooms and a knob of butter, then add asparagus, diced potato and carrot. Season and turn over in pan a few times for even cooking.

7. Cut lobster body into medallions and remove joints from claws.
8. Put a film of oil in a sauté pan. When hot add monkfish medallions. Cook for about 2 minutes on one side then turn over and cook on the other side for 1 minute.
9. Put lobster meat in a double boiler or steamer to warm through.
10. Bring lobster sauce back to a simmer.

To serve:
11. Place a cutter or ring about 3 1/2" (90mm) diameter on centre of warm serving plate. Using slotted spoon, pile mushroom/vegetable mixture into ring, gently pressing down. Remove cutter and repeat with other plates.
12. Place 3 medallions of monkfish alternately with 3 pieces of lobster around the vegetables.
13. Pour or spoon warm lobster sauce around and serve immediately.

Note:
Most of the preparation can be done in advance with only steps 6–13 being done at the last minute. This dish should be served in early summer when asparagus and wild mushrooms are both available although the vegetables can be altered to suit seasons.

Steve Davis

My favourite recipe
is a cheese, bacon and marmite sandwich
on brown bread!

Frankie Vaughan

Baked Fish
(serves 4)

2 large cod or haddock skinned fillets
2 large onions, sliced
salt and pepper

knobs of margarine
3 large carrots, sliced
milk

Put fish and vegetables in a casserole.
Cover with milk, season, top with margarine, and bake in a slow oven for 3–4 hours.

Sue Townsend

A. Mole's Scones

The warm scent of home baking does not greet me as I enter the kitchen. So I create my own smell by baking scones. Here is my recipe but remember before you rush for pencil and paper that the recipe is copyright and owned by me, Adrian Mole. So, should you wish to bake scones to this recipe then you will need to send money to me, or, in this particular case, you could send it to Cancer Research Campaign instead.

Ingredients:
4 oz flour or metric equivalent
2 oz butter or metric equivalent
2 oz sugar or metric equivalent
1 egg (eggs are still only eggs)

Method:
Beat up all the ingredients.
Make a tin greasy, throw it all in.
Turn oven to number 5.
Wait until scones are higher than they were.
Should be 12 minutes,
but keep opening oven door every 30
seconds.

Salad Dressing

Lorna Stewart

Mix together:
8 tsp sugar
8 tsp made mustard (level)
2 tsp salt (level)
good sprinkling of black pepper

In another bowl, mix with a whisk:
16 tbsp salad oil
8 dsrtsp vinegar (white)

CENSORED

Christopher Cassell

Then put a bit of the second mixture to the first and whisk,
and then the rest and mix well.

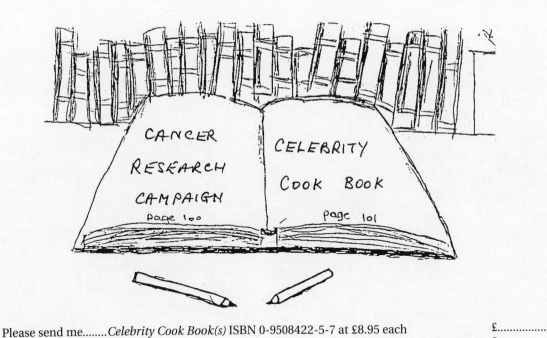

Please send me........*Celebrity Cook Book(s)* ISBN 0-9508422-5-7 at £8.95 each   £................
plus p&p at £1.25 per book   £................
     TOTAL £................

I enclose a cheque or postal order, payable to CRC Promotions Ltd, for £................
or
Please charge my credit card £................

Card type: Visa/ Access/ Mastercard/ American Express/ Switch (delete as appropriate)

Other:..(please Specify)   Issue no:................(Switch only)

Card no: _ _ _ _   _ _ _ _   _ _ _ _   _ _ _ _   Expiry date: _ _ / _ _

Name   ....

Address ....

....

....Tel: ....

Please send your order and payment to Celebrity Cook Book, CRC Promotions Ltd,
10 Cambridge Terrace, London NW1 4JL.

Thank you for buying this *Celebrity Cook Book* and supporting the work of Cancer Research Campaign.
Thanks to the generosity of our sponsors, all profits from the sale of this book are covenanted to the
Campaign and go straight into our support for pioneering cancer research. If you would like more
information about the Cancer Research Campaign please tick this box ☐

CRC Promotions Ltd Registerd Company No 2564148
Cancer Research Campaign Registered Charity No 225838

Rebecca Still